Six Figure Management Method

Six Figure Management Method

How to grow your business with the only six KPIs you'll ever need

Patrick M Georges
with Josephine Hus

KoganPage

LONDON PHILADELPHIA NEW DELHI

First published in Great Britain and the United States in 2013 by Kogan Page Limited

120 Pentonville Road
London N1 9JN
United Kingdom
www.koganpage.com

1518 Walnut Street, Suite 1100
Philadelphia PA 19102
USA

4737/23 Ansari Road
Daryaganj
New Delhi 110002
India

© Patrick M Georges 2013

The right of Patrick M Georges to be identified as the author of this work has been asserted by him in accordance with the Copyright, Designs and Patents Act 1988.

ISBN   978 0 7494 6907 8
E-ISBN   978 0 7494 6908 5

British Library Cataloguing-in-Publication Data

A CIP record for this book is available from the British Library.

Library of Congress Cataloging-in-Publication Data

Georges, Patrick M, 1953-
  Six figure management method : how to grow your business with the only six KPIs you'll ever need / Patrick M Georges, Josephine Hus.
    pages cm
  Includes bibliographical references and index.
  ISBN 978-0-7494-6907-8 – ISBN 978-0-7494-6908-5 (ebook)   1. Performance technology.
2. Organizational effectiveness. 3. Management. I. Hus, Josephine. II. Title.
  HF5549.5.P37G46 2013
  658–dc23
                                                                        2013000870

Typeset by Graphicraft Limited, Hong Kong
Printed and bound in India by Replika Press Pvt Ltd

'Simplicity applies to measurement also.
Too often we measure everything and understand nothing.'

JACK WELCH

CONTENTS

05 Do the same thing but with reduced costs and delays: measuring and improving your gains from processes performance 123

06 Give more to the best people: measuring and improving your people responsibility level performance 149

07   Invest more in your critical resource: measuring and improving your return on critical resource performance   169

08   Focus on one key change project: measuring and improving your key project status performance   189

ABOUT THE AUTHORS

Patrick M Georges is a professor in management. He teaches at some of the leading European MBA schools, including HEC Paris, Collège des Ingénieurs and the University of Brussels. A serial entrepreneur, he has successfully created and sold several companies. He developed the Management Cockpit, the most used business performance room methodology worldwide. He is the author of numerous best-sellers, including *Increase Your Effectiveness* and *The Management Cockpit: Essential Scoreboards*. As a medical doctor and brain surgeon, he is the former head of the neurosurgery department at the University Medical Centre Vesale in Belgium. Contact: **pgeorges@arcadis.be**.

Josephine Hus was born in New York and has an MSc in Electronics. She is an engineer with an MBA from Collège des Ingénieurs. She has extensive experience with 4G wireless technologies, has worked in performance management within Airbus and is now a management consultant at a major strategy consulting firm.

FOREWORD

Mastering performance, especially in a crisis period, is a key concern for companies, their leaders and their managers. Measured, monitored and managed at different levels of the organization as well as at the individual level, performance is one of the drivers that brings momentum to a company. Performance management should therefore be considered not just as a managerial technique, but rather as a managerial act.

This is how Patrick M Georges and Josephine Hus approach performance management. Firstly, by associating performance management with the leader or the manager confronted with a multitude of strategic and operational decisions and, secondly, by illustrating the dialectical link between strategy and performance, the book addresses managing performance less as a 'system' that reflects strategy than as a set of reasoned questions that contribute to shaping it.

The authors' approach is also guided by a desire for simplicity. We expect a lot from a system that measures and manages performance: to clarify strategy and translate strategic objectives into measurable indicators, communicate strategy and improve alignment across the organization, plan, set targets and enhance feedback and learning on results achieved, and so on. This complexity calls for simplicity. The underlying motivation of *Six Figure Management Method* is to encourage reflection. Turning its back on 'ready-made' models, it invites readers to question their strategy and its critical drivers towards superior performance.

Karine Le Joly, Director of Academic Innovation
and Coordination, HEC Executive Education, Paris

PREFACE

As managers, educators or consultants, we like to believe that the world of business and management is complicated: more of an art than a science, and very complex, with interwoven challenges and opportunities, embedded knowledge, unknown territory, and impossible-to-predict scenarios. And it is a difficult-to-understand world, as any human endeavour is, but perhaps we create some of this complexity ourselves. Perhaps we enjoy the fact that many are mystified by management.

In this book the authors seek not so much to demystify but rather to render the act of successfully running a company manageable, taking what is inherently difficult and unpredictable, and providing leaders and their teams with simple indicators that will increase their chances of success. Business is a relative game; all one needs to do is outperform the competition and the market and, using the authors' suggestion of six key factors, your chances of doing this are increased greatly. This book provides not only a way of doing that, but also practical examples and suggestions.

Why am I writing this preface? What struck me about this book? My favourite article on strategy is 'Are you sure you have a strategy?' by D C Hambrick and J W Fredrickson (*Academy of Management Executive*, **15** (4), 2001). Why? Because it gives managers a simple, solid and coherent framework to see their world and guide them as they make difficult decisions on a day-to-day basis. The authors of this book have done the same thing. And, without diminishing Hambrick and Fredrickson, they have gone one step further: in addition to proposing six key factors, they have shown how managers can discover the six factors that matter to them and their business, and they've done it in a way that any manager or employee can understand. They've made management manageable, and they've shown how easily, if you enjoyed Hambrick and Fredrickson as much as I did, you can link your organization's six key factors to your firm's strategy.

Of the six factors that they propose, let's look at time facing customers. Measuring how much time the company or key individuals spend with clients would seem to be fundamental to most businesses, but we've all seen examples of firms that seem to have forgotten this. How can you find the business, or know what innovations your future clients need, or respond to problems (or even know problems exist) if you aren't spending significant time with clients?

Or consider the people responsibility level. How many companies, or for that matter how many leaders, have a target for the autonomy of their key employees? I am trying to remember the last time I met a senior executive who mentioned in a serious way the effort he or she put into helping more direct reports be responsible for a bigger piece of the business, or gauged how well he or she was delegating to well-prepared, proud and responsible employees, or (outside the human resource department) had a clear idea of the high-potential individuals who were ready to move up in the organization. I believe just this section of the book alone makes it worth reading and reflecting on.

Another aspect of this book that I appreciated was that you can use the authors' approach for the whole company or just for the part of it for which you are responsible. The choice and design of the six factors are up to you, the responsible manager. Everything here is in your hands.

On reading this book some might argue that the authors have tried to make the running of an organization too simple, or even simplistic. That reminds me of a phrase I've often heard: 'Make sure your company is so easy to run that an idiot can do it, as one day an idiot will.' No one reading this book is an idiot, but the point is well taken. Ensure that in times of stress or change, or with managers who aren't as competent as one would like, the company can be run efficiently, and that everyone knows what the key indicators are that they have to focus on. The authors have done a magnificent job of showing us how to do this. And doing it starts with you.

Jim Pulcrano,
Executive Director, IMD, Switzerland

ACKNOWLEDGEMENTS

To the leading academic authorities Michel Badoc and Bertrand Moingeon, HEC Paris, Philippe Mahrer, Collège des Ingénieurs, Paris, and Bruno van Pottelsberghe, Solvay Brussels School, for permission and encouragement to teach at their prestigious business schools.

To top executives Hasso Plattner and Henning Kagermann at SAP, the leading enterprise software company, and Grégoire Talbot, CEO of Cockpit Group, for their permission and encouragement to conduct a survey with their many customers worldwide.

To Pierre-Alain Cardinaux, partner at Ernst & Young, Switzerland, for his help in writing the French version of this book.

To William Q Judge, E V Williams Chair of Strategic Leadership, Editor, *Corporate Governance: An International Review*, Old Dominion University, Norfolk, VA, who with great patience helped us to make this book better.

A special thanks to Liz Gooster, Editor-at-Large at Kogan Page, for helping us to turn our research and academic notes into a readable book.

Executive summary

The six figure management method is simple, proved and universal. Any organization can succeed if it measures and improves only a few carefully selected key performance indicators (KPIs). The six figure method has proved that, if you measure and improve only six well-selected figures, the profitability of your unit will soar.

These six figures are the guiding stars in the management of your activities, providing goals and leadership. They direct you towards high financial performance through down-to-earth motivation levers. These levers consist of operational parameters of the business that attract significantly more employee attention than financial results, which are too abstract to relate to. However, these levers systematically drive your business to financial success. The six figure method enables managers to thrive at all levels of the organization, in all sectors, private or public.

According to our research work, the six KPIs to improve are:

- *Sales from new sources (SFN)*, the growth indicator, which measures your innovation performance. Increase your income, sales, budgets and orders from new sources: products, customers, processes and channels.
- *Time facing customers (TFC)*, the heading indicator, which measures your customer orientation performance. Increase your time, interface and interactions facing your customers, internal or external.

- *Gains from processes (GFP)*, the power indicator, which measures your operational excellence performance. Increase your gains from improved processes.

- *People responsibility level (PRL)*, the attitude indicator, which measures your employee orientation performance. Increase the responsibility of your key people.

- *Return on critical resource (RCR)*, the speed indicator, which measures your profitability performance. Improve the returns, profits and occupation rates of your most critical resources: cash, people and technologies.

- *Key project status (KPS)*, the coordination indicator, which measures your leadership performance. Improve the status and deliverables of your most important change project.

The missing link between finance and people

Six figure management (SFM) is a business management strategy originally developed in 2009 by decision sciences expert Patrick M Georges, well known from his creation of the Management Cockpit, the favourite executive decision room worldwide. It seeks to help managers to reach a sustainable growth for their organization, private or public, small or large, profit or non-profit, by measuring and improving six carefully selected organization performance areas.

Patrick M Georges's research findings are based on a 10-year study with more than 975 organizations, searching for a link between the improvement of certain key performance indicators and the sustainable growth of the organization.

This new management method is striking in its simplicity, universality and scalability from a one-person organization to a business unit to the largest corporation. It is an action and motivation plan and not just another measurement system. It's a growth engine more than a growth scoreboard. To achieve its results, SFM activates a set of management methods to optimize those six performance areas. It creates a special structure of dashboards in the organization and engages an SFM project carried out in the organization that follows a defined sequence and has quantified targets for the six sustainable growth drivers.

This action and motivation plan is carried out by all the employees throughout the organization through INDIRA, a new enterprise social network with management-by-objective capabilities. INDIRA is a trademark of NEURO Cognitive Sciences. For more information visit **www.indiraweb.com** or contact **pgeorges@arcadis.be.**

Introduction: how to thrive, simply

KEY LEARNING POINTS

- How to improve the efficiency of your organization while striving for simplicity.

- The six figures that are truly important for measuring and improving your organization.

- Why these six figures are important in today's business world.

- The dimensions that benefit from this method, from improving your organization to improving the performance of your team and yourself as a manager.

Why we are writing this book

We want to share with you our astonishing research results: only six performance indicators are needed in order to clearly predict the success of any organization. We will demonstrate that throughout this book. We will show you how to benefit from this discovery for yourself, your team and your organization.

Who can benefit?

This book addresses a wide range of readers, from managers responsible for very small businesses to CEOs of large corporations, in both the private and the public sector.

What do we want you to do?

1 Decide to improve your performance now, because it's easy and straightforward with this method.

2 Find the six indicators that fit your situation. We will provide you with many clues along the way.

3 Measure, display and delegate improvement with these indicators.

What do we mean by six figure management?

Six figure management (SFM) is a simple performance management method where managers simply use *six figures* to measure the six key performance areas that drive a business towards sustainable and profitable growth, keeping the business focused on the missing link between people's activities and financial results.

A figure is a relevant measurement for a target to reach at a precise date, and can be:

- a number;
- a level on a scale;
- a deliverable;
- a fact that an independent observer can verify.

It goes under different names in the literature:

- measure;
- key performance indicator (KPI);

- critical success factor (CSF);
- business performance indicator.

How to thrive, simply: as a manager, a team leader or a businessperson

A surprising discovery has emerged both from brain research and from the hard data of more than 960 enterprises: any organization can thrive by simply measuring and improving a set of only six key performance indicators.

Keep it simple

Many business books present key performance indicators as a multitude of business ratios to measure and monitor. Many managers have lost their way in this profusion. We focus on the six essentials, ignoring many indicators to concentrate on the few that are critical and universal.

We ignore the financial ratios. They will follow suit if the six KPIs, or six figures we recommend, are in the green zone. We ignore the operational factors. First-line managers and employees will take care of them if you show the way with your six figures.

The SFM method has the guts to state that only six well-defined performance indicators need be monitored in order to thrive. It claims that they are universal, and has proved it with many case studies at different levels in organizations. The truth is that management consists of a small number of essential measures and improvements by means of which managers can appraise the success of any organization.

The six figures that we propose to managers are operational enough to motivate people. They are result-oriented enough to execute a strategy. Each figure in itself is easy to calculate, and it is simple to understand what each means. The six figures mesh together to give managers the big picture about the health and future of their organizations. Managers want to become familiar with this method, because it is the one that will have most impact on their responsibilities in the future.

Many books and seminars sell advice on management to managers. They contain page after page of complex theories, vague concepts and general, unspecific recommendations. This book is a practical handbook for all managers, packed with easy-to-apply, down-to-earth tips and techniques.

Managers fulfil six key functions

1 *Managers innovate.* In the SFM method, this function is measured by their sales from new sources (SFN) performance.

2 *Managers satisfy the customer, internal or external.* In the SFM method, this function is measured by their time facing customers (TFC) performance.

3 *Managers reduce costs and delays at target quality levels.* In the SFM method, this function is measured by their gains from processes (GFP) performance.

4 *Managers delegate to the best people.* In the SFM method, this function is measured by their people responsibility level (PRL) performance.

5 *Managers return what they receive with a profit.* In the SFM method, this function is measured by their return on critical resource (RCR) performance.

6 *Managers adapt to changes.* In the SFM method, this function is measured by their key project status (KPS) performance.

CASE STUDY 0.1

Who

Liza is a senior manager with eight years of experience in a top US consumer goods company. She started her career as a junior marketing manager in a European unit. She has now become head of the body care unit of the company, with more than 5,000 employees worldwide. The board has given her the opportunity to get to grips with the entire business.

Why

Liza decided first to select the right questions to ask the functional executives and the right metrics for evaluating their work. She studied the systems for 360-degree performance review and finally selected the six figure process to evaluate the work of all the functional executives as the best simple template to systematically list the most important KPIs to track.

How

Liza asked each of her team members:

- are you increasing customer numbers and sales of new products?

- are you increasing your time and interaction with customers?

- are you reducing your costs and delays at a stable quality level?

- are you giving more responsibilities to your high-potential managers?

- are you improving the return on your most critical resources: our research results?

- what is the current status of our most critical project: the sustainability project?

CASE STUDY 0.2

Who

John-Paul is the CEO of a large mining company. He wanted to shake things up at his company and lead it as a socially driven company. He has a scoreboard for a business model aimed at contributing to society and the environment based on the six figure process for improvement.

Why

John-Paul wanted his idea to be hard-wired and linked to the bottom line. He wanted sustainability to benefit the business.

How

- By increasing sales from new sources and sustainable supply.

- By increasing time facing customers as the community social leaders.

- By increasing gains from processes through reduced waste and pollution.

- By increasing the people responsibility level through executive reward on a reduced environmental footprint.

- By increasing the return on critical resource through the volume generated by each unit of energy consumed.

- By improving the key project status of the social responsibility project.

CASE STUDY 0.3

Who

Sven is the chief operating officer of a large Scandinavian furniture company.

Why

'I want to extend the network with a new type of town-centre shop', Sven stated during his quarterly speech.

How

- Sales from new points of sale at 10 per cent of total sales.
- Time facing critical customers: the city authorities: two visits per week.
- Gains from processes: all new shops should use 20 per cent less energy per square metre.
- People responsibility level: shop managers should be rapidly responsible for more shops, on performance.
- Return on critical resource: profitability per square metre.
- Key project status: new sales channel project on time and on budget.

CASE STUDY 0.4

Who

Ron is the international business developer in charge of franchising the brand of a famous East Coast hospital in the Middle East.

Why

Joining forces with a local partner in Saudi Arabia, Ron plans to include a six figure scoreboard in the franchising contract to motivate franchisees to strengthen their advisory position and follow their patient quality care guidelines. Lending the brand name to local partners that deliver care below average can damage the brand. At the first stage of franchising, Ron wants to focus on quality, not financial results.

How

- Strategic objective: attract more wealthy patients to finance the non-profitable activities.
    - SFN indicator: revenues from new target patients at 15 per cent.
    - Management control: increase the marketing budget by 3 per cent.
    - Accountable manager: Khaled.

- Strategic objective: get doctors closer to their patients.
    - TFC indicator: time facing patients at a minimum of 30 minutes per day.
    - Management control: decrease doctors' paperwork time thanks to bedside computers.
    - Accountable manager: Ihram.

- Strategic objective: transmit quality patient care know-how to the franchisee.
    - GFP indicator: deviances from care processes less than 15 per cent.
    - Management control: adapt the processes to the local culture and test them in pilot units managed by US executives.
    - Accountable manager: Ibn Sour.

- Strategic objective: get the best local executives to replace the US executives as fast as possible.
  - PRL indicator: percentage of local executives in charge.
  - Management control: rank local executives according to the management review committee criteria.
  - Accountable manager: Asham.
- Strategic objective: increase the bed occupancy rate.
  - RCR indicator: return on capital invested per bed.
  - Management control: train local executive to use the resource allocation software.
  - Accountable manager: Adam.
- Strategic objective: delegate the CEO position to a local CEO.
  - KPS indicator: quarterly deliverables on time and on specification.
  - Management control: increase Ron's staff by two associates before the end of the year.
  - Accountable manager: Ron.

How this book will help you

The SFM method is a guideline for building and maintaining profitable business. It will also make your life at work much easier. Whatever your role, this book will teach you how to successfully measure, monitor and manage your unit, your team or even your own personal activity by using a performance dashboard.

The business literature is packed with books on performance management. However, these books convey a theoretical approach to performance management, leaving executives and managers with the difficult task of scaling and applying the methods to organizations. *Six Figure Management Method* is the first straightforward manual on performance management offering the reader a simple and applicable approach to create value in business.

Through extensive research work, we have demonstrated that the key to good management and growing a business is simply a matter of measuring and improving six carefully chosen indicators that must be included in your organization's dashboard. If you measure and optimize them, your business will be successful.

The proposed method is simple to implement but certainly not simplistic, as it provides a complete 360-degree view of your organization's performance. The six figures refer to the key performance indicators that ensure a balanced survey of your business: sales from new sources, time facing customers, gains from processes, people responsibility level, return on critical resource, and key project status.

The six figure method

The SFM method provides a simple, straightforward, easy-to-learn and efficient method proven to enhance your business performance, no matter what size your organization is, from a big corporation to a small start-up, and whether it is in the private or the public sector. You can easily scale this method to practically any type of activity that involves management, including your own personal career.

This book is meant for anyone looking to enhance their managerial skills, from experienced CEOs and unit managers to employees monitoring their own day-to-day activities. It also has high applicability to diverse situations outside business or to those in the public sphere: a mayor running a city, a doctor in charge of a medical unit, an engineer supervising a technical unit and so on. The chapters are packed with simple tips and techniques to improve your management performance. The book is the first of its kind to offer a highly practical performance management method with universal applicability. Step-by-step guidelines are provided.

The book will give you fast and efficient management tools without the need for additional training or for acquiring extensive management knowledge. If you already have a management background, this book will provide you with some fresh ideas and structure on how to effectively improve your business.

Tools for each of the six measures

- A list of the most effective indicators to measure performance.
- A list of favourite methods to improve performance.
- A list of examples of different implementations of this method.
- A checklist of questions to ask yourself.
- A step-by-step implementation programme.
- Managers' testimonials.

Testimonial sources and research background

Our last five years of academic courses have been dedicated to the management methods presented here. These courses were taught in different universities and business schools throughout Europe and the United States to managers and executives from both the public and the private sector. These managers and executives brought significant contributions, which we've incorporated into this book as examples.

Why the six figure management method uses these six KPIs

Thanks to our exposure to more than 1,000 company installations over 10 years, we have had privileged access to KPIs used by different organizations over long periods of time. We have correlated the main indicators that these companies have chosen to measure and improve with the results the companies achieved month after month. Our conclusion was that successful organizations, regardless of the measure of success that they've achieved, are the ones that measure the six performance indicators that we describe in this book.

This executive survey was carried out for more than 15 years. It was conducted worldwide with all types of organizations, small and large, public and private. The survey was possible thanks to the connection of one of the authors, Patrick M Georges, with SAP, the giant enterprise software company. We conducted the study at the offices of SAP Palo Alto and Philadelphia for the United States, Tokyo and Shanghai for Asia, and London, Paris and Walldorf for Europe, asking hundreds of executives the same question: what are your favourite six figures to grow your organization?

The study was carried out from 1 June 1989 to 29 July 2007 with the examination of 975 'scoreboards' from different organizations. The study was widely facilitated by Patrick M Georges's role as the inventor of the Management Cockpit, now owned by the Cockpit Group, a dashboard system particularly appreciated around the world for its ergonomics. Patrick M Georges personally supervised over 200 performance measurement systems in many company units, some of the best known of which are IBM, Microsoft, SAP, Accor and AXA. As a partner of the corporate software giant SAP for 10 years, he had access to the scorecards of many companies. During business performance measurement training sessions, the authors were able to ask many managers anonymously which six numbers they used to pilot their unit.

In 1989, three years before the publication of 'The balanced scorecard' by Kaplan and Norton (1992), we installed the first Management Cockpit (MC) at Crédit Suisse, a major international bank. Eleven years later, in 2000, a study of the 50 first MC cases was published by *Wirtschaftsinformatik*, the leading German management IT magazine. Four years later, the first 150 MC dashboards were analysed in a reference book in France. The six numbers of the SFM method were already beginning to emerge as growth predictors for organizations in this publication. By 2010, there were 975 cases in the knowledge base.

Over a period of five years, we ranked the surveyed organizations as successful, stable or lagging, based on the results they displayed on the 'Will we reach our objectives?' panel in their MC room. Then we correlated this ranking with the six KPIs they displayed on the 'Will we thrive?' panel in their room. This panel is designed to show what are, for them, the six main causal factors for the green and red lamps on the 'Will we reach our objectives?' panel. We found out that the organizations that displayed on their 'Are we thriving?' panel the six KPIs that we now promote as the SFM method are also those with the most green lamps on their main 'Will we reach our objectives?' panel.

When we looked at the category of 'growing companies', we identified 35 of the most frequent business performance measurements. From these, managers' favourite choices for the indicators to display on their main dashboard, 'How are our key growth factors?', were:

- Performance 1: sales from new sources type of indicators;
- Performance 10: time facing customers type of indicators;
- Performance 14: gains from processing type of indicators;
- Performance 19: people responsibility level type of indicators;
- Performance 29: return on critical resource type of indicators;
- Performance 33: key project status type of indicators.

See Figure 0.1.

FIGURE 0.1   Favourite choices of indicators

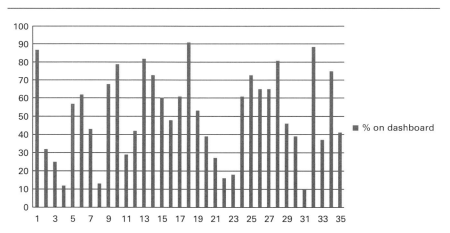

A simple and proven method to improve your results

The basic idea is to select the key indicators that best describe your performance from all perspectives, monitor them and then set and apply corrective actions in order to improve. The choice of indicators might seem like common sense, but it is actually difficult to identify them by yourself. Home-made solutions that organizations come up with are too often proven to fail. This book is the result of in-depth research and has already been successfully tested by numerous managers. Six figure management provides a fast and efficient method that can be implemented in three easy steps:

1 You decide, with the help of this book, which are the six major performance indicators for your activity.

2 You measure and monitor your performance and you establish a set of target objectives in order to improve your current performance.

3 You apply a set of proven methods to achieve your targets. They are described in each chapter directly or through comments from seminar participants.

The six figures

Our recommendation is to measure, monitor and improve the following six figures that are currently the key success factors of many managers and organizations:

- SFN: sales from new sources;
- TFC: time facing customers;
- GFP: gains from processes;
- PRL: people responsibility level;
- RCR: return on critical resource;
- KPS: key project status.

In order to ensure a complete and balanced performance, your organization must simultaneously measure, monitor and improve the capacity to:

1 innovate, change and adapt: sales from new sources performance;

2 market, enlarge its audience and satisfy its clients: time facing customers performance;

3 minimize costs and delays without compromising quality: gains from processes performance;

4 satisfy the needs and increase the responsibility and autonomy of your best people: people responsibility level performance;

5 take care of its main resources and make good use of its capital and resources in general: return on critical resource performance;

6 manage the progress of key activities effectively: key project status performance.

These figures will describe your unit's progress and can be directly enhanced by following some simple tips and techniques, which are described in the following chapters.

The methods described do not require you to be a strategy guru. Moreover, they convey a structured approach to improve your activity without relying on hazardous actions or luck.

In this book, each of the six figures is explained in detail, and performance improvement methods are proposed. Choose and customize these six figures to improve your activity and boost your business!

Testimonial: The CEO of
a large Shanghai computer company

'6, 6, 6, 6, 6 and 6. Those are my magical six figures.

For this year, SFN: +6 per cent.

TFC: +6 countries where our products should be available.

GFP: –6 per cent costs by subcontracting our screen manufacturing.

PRL: double the budget in the charge of six high-potential managers per subsidiary.

RCR: 6 per cent.

KPS: six green lamps for the six key deliverables on time.'

Testimonial: An executive at
a UK jet engine manufacturing company

'Here we compare our SFM method to a jet engine providing the climb thrust we need to grow our business. We get the best air intake thanks to our SFN and TFC performance, excellent compression and combustion thanks to our GFP and PRL performance, and the resulting exhaust climb thrust through RCR and KPS.'

What is the origin of the term 'six figure management'?

'Six figure management' was coined by Patrick M Georges from executives saying 'Back to basics, back to the six figures that should pilot our organization.'

Can the public sector and non-profit organizations also benefit from the six figure management method?

All organizations can take advantage of SFM. Improving results and effectiveness is a clear goal for all organizations. Here is a typical translation used by the public sector: sales from new sources becomes budgets from new sources and donations from new partnerships; time facing customers becomes time facing citizens; and so on.

Profitable growth is the main goal of many organizations, public or private. Financial profitability is the goal for the private sector, while social profitability is the goal for the public sector. The six indicators work together, balanced or linked, towards this main goal (see Figure 0.2).

FIGURE 0.2   Working together

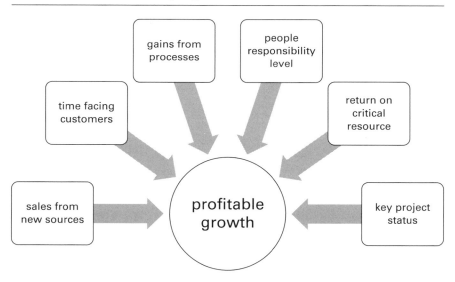

FIGURE 0.3   Employees' best driver per goal

Goal	Employees' best driver
Innovation	Sales from new sources
Customers' satisfaction	Time facing customers
Operational excellence	Gains from processes
People motivation	People responsibility level
Profitability	Return on critical resource
Leadership	Key project status

Investing in a new scorecard method will never be fully profitable if the scorecard doesn't clearly speak to employees; it has to call to action and to change. The six indicators of SFM are operational indicators; they are real people movers, driving employees to change their behaviours (see Figure 0.3).

Frequently asked questions

Why only six figures?

- Your memory is already highly employed. Six figures are easy to remember and to grasp at a single glance.
- The status of your business has to be simple and comprehensible to everyone.

- Having a clear improvement strategy strengthens your position and credibility as a leader.

- Clear and concise objectives motivate everyone.

- Good managers base their activity on a few strong and simple principles.

- If these six indicators are green, you can be sure that you are improving your performance.

- If some indicators are red, you know exactly where to concentrate your efforts.

Why is this method efficient?

- It is simple and easy to apply. It is based on common sense and on the collective experience of numerous organizations over a long period of time.

- These six figures are carefully selected and tested by management specialists and require only adaptation to your own situation.

- There is no need to hire expensive consultants in order to understand and apply this methodology.

- It is intuitive and highly motivating.

- It does not require a great level of effort to implement, as it merely consists of structuring and processing the data that you already have, and reporting it on a recurrent basis.

- Knowing your strengths and weaknesses precisely is a competitive advantage.

- It increases awareness of threats and opportunities throughout the organization.

- It increases corporate culture and solidarity among employees.

How often should the measurements be performed?

Once every quarter is usually enough to grasp your performance. However, it is recommended that you keep track of your results in order to trace your performance through time.

Will I be able to gather the data for my measurements?

This is not a problem. The required information usually already exists in your enterprise resource planning, whether it's SAP, Oracle or any other database infrastructure. However, if this is not this case, the information can still easily be collected.

If you don't have the required data and if the respective indicator is of high strategic importance for your activity, you must in any case perform the measurement. The chapters for each indicator describe simple tips and techniques to create, find or measure the related performance.

What are the dangers of this method?

Important improvements do not come without risks. Each chapter contains a description of frequent mistakes that can jeopardize the efficiency of the method behind each of these six figures.

Should I decide by myself or together with my team?

Always engage your team in the decision process. However, be aware that it is your responsibility to come up with a convincing proposition.

What should I do with the other indicators that I receive?

Delegate any other indicators to lower levels of management or specific teams: finance, marketing, human resources and project management. These six key performance indicators are mutually exclusive and collectively exhaustive regarding your organization's overall performance.

Should I publish my results for anyone in the organization to see?

Yes, as much as you can. Employees and managers must all be aligned and motivated by the same common objectives. Ideas for improvement can come from within the organization, so you have to make sure that awareness is high.

I'm a manager in the public sector. Will this method help me?

Yes, this method is universal and fits any organization aiming to succeed and serve its public better. Just change the vocabulary: replace 'sales' with 'budget' or 'resources', 'customers' with 'citizens' or 'taxpayers' and the like.

How should I use this book?

Read this book and organize a one- or two-day seminar with your team in order to adapt the method to your business. Do not adjourn the seminar without making sure that you have all agreed not only on the six figures of your organization's performance but also on the corresponding target values.

Then organize a dedicated project for this activity, name the person in charge and set about implementation. Dedicated seminars and software solutions are available for you to make the six figure method a simple, plug-in solution for your organization.

Can the six figure management method help you?

Are you a first-line manager in a small business unit? Are you an executive heading a large strategic business unit? Do you work in public administration? Do you run a service line? Do you run a small shop? Are you a young manager? You can take advantage of the SFM method.

To convince you, just have a look at Tables 0.1 to 0.8, which show the scoreboards of several organizations, large and small, private and public, profit and non-profit. People who have built scoreboards into their companies have simply decided to thrive, to move on, to improve their results and to grow their organization.

TABLE 0.1   A business unit of a large ICT corporation

Measure	Result
Sales from new sources (innovation results performance)	Percentage of sales of new products, to new customers and through new processes, brought to the level of the main competitor.
Time facing customers (customer closeness performance)	Increase of 10 per cent in the hours per day that a salesperson passes on average in front of new prospects.
Gains from processes (operational excellence performance)	Reduction in costs of 2 per cent for activity A by automation.
People responsibility level (people motivation performance)	Increase of 10 per cent in the pay-for-performance compensation of high-potential employees.
Return on critical resource (key profitability performance)	Increase of 4 per cent in the benefit per key manager.
Key project status (leadership performance)	Next deliverable on time and on specification for the most critical project this quarter.

TABLE 0.2   The executive committee at a mid-size oil company

Measure	Result
Sales from new sources (innovation results performance)	Part of the sales revenues acquired through a new distribution partnership.
Time facing customers (customer closeness performance)	Increase in the time spent with critical shareholders and investors of one meeting per month.
Gains from processes (operational excellence performance)	Improvements on the strategic plan milestones through the implementation of a new software system.
People responsibility level (people motivation performance)	Increase in the variable compensation of executives.
Return on critical resource (key profitability performance)	Increase in the return on the most costly capital of 3 per cent.
Key project status (leadership performance)	Next deliverable on time and on specification for the most critical project this quarter.

TABLE 0.3   A young manager at an Italian fashion company

Measure	Result
Sales from new sources (innovation results performance)	Percentage of income obtained thanks to new competences acquired studying for MBA.
Time facing customers (customer closeness performance)	Increase in hours per week spent with the company owner and hours spent with family.
Gains from processes (operational excellence performance)	Reduction in delays in the production of reports through mastering the new software for design support.
People responsibility level (people motivation performance)	Increase in budget and people in the area of responsibility.
Return on critical resource (key profitability performance)	Increase in income per worked day.
Key project status (leadership performance)	Next deliverable on time and on specification for the most critical project this quarter.

TABLE 0.4   The White House

Measure	Result
Sales from new sources (innovation results performance)	Percentage of budget shifted from public spending A to public spending B.
Time facing customers (customer closeness performance)	Increase in time spent by executives with critical representatives.
Gains from processes (operational excellence performance)	Reduction of 10 per cent in delays in decision-making processes A, B and C by elimination of steps X and Z.
People responsibility level (people motivation performance)	Increase of 5 per cent in the discretionary budgets of employees.
Return on critical resource (key profitability performance)	Available time increased by 10 per cent for issue C.
Key project status (leadership performance)	Next deliverable on time and on specification for the most critical project this quarter.

TABLE 0.5   A hospital in Switzerland

Measure	Result
Sales from new sources (innovation results performance)	Percentage of activities carried out for the benefit of categories of patients that could not be helped three years earlier.
Time facing customers (customer closeness performance)	Increase of 10 per cent in the hours per week spent with referring physicians by the appropriate personnel.
Gains from processes (operational excellence performance)	Reduction in hospital infections of 2 per cent, by penalties being doubled for deviances from the relevant processes.
People responsibility level (people motivation performance)	Increase of 25 per cent in responsibility for results for the heads of the hospital's responsibility centres.
Return on critical resource (key profitability performance)	Increase of 4 per cent in average activities invoiced per bed.
Key project status (leadership performance)	Next deliverable on time and on specification for the most critical project this quarter.

TABLE 0.6   The mayor of a city in Germany

Measure	Result
Sales from new sources (innovation results performance)	Percentage of the budget obtained from new sources, eg ecological taxes and regional subsidies.
Time facing customers (customer closeness performance)	Increase of 10 per cent in the opening hours of critical public services.
Gains from processes (operational excellence performance)	Reduction in costs of 5 per cent thanks to e-administration and citizens' self-administration.
People responsibility level (people motivation performance)	Increase of 3 per cent in pay-for-performance compensation.
Return on critical resource (key profitability performance)	Increase of 4 per cent in the utilization rate of underused public infrastructure.
Key project status (leadership performance)	Next deliverable on time and on specification for the most critical project this quarter.

TABLE 0.7   A Rotary club in the UK

Measure	Result
Sales from new sources (innovation results performance)	Improvement of 10 per cent in the percentage of members with a membership of less than five years.
Time facing customers (customer closeness performance)	Increase of 10 per cent in the hours per month that members give in service to their local community.
Gains from processes (operational excellence performance)	Increase of 5 per cent in amount collected per hour spent on fundraising activities.
People responsibility level (people motivation performance)	Increase in the rate of participation by members on committees.
Return on critical resource (key profitability performance)	Increase in amount of social action by members of the club.
Key project status (leadership performance)	Next deliverable on time and on specification for the most critical project this quarter.

TABLE 0.8 A retail shop on the US East Coast

Measure	Result
Sales from new sources (innovation results performance)	Percentage of overall sales from products on sale for less than one month.
Time facing customers (customer closeness performance)	Reduction of 10 per cent in queues.
Gains from processes (operational excellence performance)	Deviance of less than 5 per cent from the new purchase process.
People responsibility level (people motivation performance)	Increase of 5 per cent in payment for results for picking personnel.
Return on critical resource (key profitability performance)	Result per square metre up by 6 per cent.
Key project status (leadership performance)	Next deliverable on time and on specification for the most critical project this quarter.

Six figure management in action
How we know it really works

01

> **KEY LEARNING POINT**
>
> - This method is based on in-depth analysis, management methods and neuro-management.

Good books and publications on performance management and key performance indicators are numerous (see Aguinis, 2009; Armstrong, 2006; Hoffmann, Lesser and Ringo, 2012; Kaplan, 2009; Lebas, 1995; Otley, 1999; Parmenter, 2009; Walsh, 1996). Advances in management control and decision sciences led to the development of the six figure management (SFM) method. Our field study confirmed that the method is a key advantage for managers and organizations seeking to improve their results.

The SFM method is a management control-based approach

One of the keys to success for managers is to develop a business model that defines how they want their organizations to be managed. A control system is essential to ensure that the model is followed. Control enables managers to focus on their organizations and keep them on track with plans. This is an important management function after decision making, planning, resource organization, and leadership (see Griffin, 2005: 651–83; Kroll *et al*, 1997; Taylor, 1994).

Control is the regulation of the organization's activities for the purpose of facilitating goal achievement. It provides necessary information about the organization's performance to managers, compared to the goals they set for themselves. It enables them to compare the current situation with the desired outcome. It indicates potential problems so that they can react and change their decisions.

One of the roles of control is to help managers deal with the complexity of their organizations. As soon as an organization has more than a few people, it becomes difficult for the human mind to track it. The control KPIs must be few in number to be useful to managers, as the human attention span is generally limited to six pieces of information. They must provide managers with an overall understanding or bird's eye view of the situation and with a good picture of the current state of the organization's four kinds of resources: human, financial, physical and information. They must provide a good understanding at the organization's four levels: process or project level, profitability level, organizational level and strategy level. The SFM method fulfils this task.

Each of the KPIs must be adaptable to a manager's situation thanks to well-chosen measurements. The measurements will vary depending on the organization's strategy, environment and potential. For example, for the innovation KPI, sales from new sources, the measurements can be 'sales from new products' or 'sales from new customers' depending on the situation of the organization.

The KPIs must be reliable and measurable on a regular basis. Experience shows that every activity can be evaluated, either by measurement or by indices whose value is sufficient to aid decision making.

Operations control

Operations control monitors the processes for transforming resources into products and services. In the SFM approach, this type of control is carried out as a 'post-action control', not earlier. It focuses on the results of well-managed operations: the cost and time savings actually obtained. The SFM method's gains from processes KPI is responsible for the task of controlling operations excellence.

Financial control

The control of financial resources is essential in all organizations, even non-profit ones. In the SFM approach, we favour the analysis of the profitability ratios of committed resources and, in particular, the profitability of the organization's most critical resource – whether this is connected to customers, value, rarity, price or competitors and regardless of whether it is a financial, human, physical or information resource. The SFM method's return on critical resource KPI is responsible for the task of controlling critical profitability.

Structural control

Two types of structural control are carried out with the SFM method. Decentralized control and employee commitment are selected over bureaucratic-type control. Structural control of the customer-orientation type is also deemed to be critical in the SFM approach. The time facing customers and people responsibility level KPIs are responsible for the task of controlling the adaptation of the organization's structure to personnel and customers. The SFM suggests, for example, that structural control consists in a regular and speedy increase in budgets entrusted to the best employees and an increase in time spent in contact with customers.

Strategic control

Strategic control ensures that the organization takes its environment into account and moves towards its goals. The sales from new sources and key performance status KPIs are responsible for the business strategy control task.

Effective control

Control is more effective if it is flexible and can quickly adapt to business and customer changes. It is more effective if it quickly informs the manager of significant changes. It is effective if measurements can be made with the least amount of distortion and manipulation possible.

We developed the six KPIs of the SFM approach with this in mind. Regardless of whether it is sales from new sources, time facing customers, gains from processes or whatever, results can be obtained quickly, on a regular basis and without distortion. They are flexible in terms of the choice of measurements used to evaluate them. For example, the gains from processes KPI can be converted from the 'cost reduction' measurement to the 'delays reduction' measurement in a flexible way while maintaining focus on operations excellence.

Coping with the dangers of management controlling

Over-control

The SFM approach deals with the danger of over-controlling all details: all activities, all movements, all delays. The SFM method focuses on the missing link between activities and results by monitoring a small number of KPIs at the inter-mediate tactical level of the organization, leaving the field open to strategic and operations initiatives above and below this level of control.

Inappropriate focus

No one can blame a management method for focusing on innovation, customers, operations excellence, personal account-ability, return on a critical resource, or the status of the key project. These are exactly the six performance areas SFM focuses on.

Why you should have only six KPIs for intelligence

More information is less intelligence

Paul Andreassen, a researcher at MIT, conducted the first re-search into how the quality of a decision related to the amount of information received by the decision maker with groups of businesspeople. In order to make a standard make-or-buy decision, a first group received only some essential information to make that decision. The second group received the same information together with additional information to make their decision. Counter-intuitively, the first group with less information ended up with better decisions, as though the additional information had distracted the second group from the essential information. This is explained by the limited ability of our prefrontal brain to handle a number of pieces of information at one time.

The human brain can handle up to six pieces of information simultaneously. If it receives more, it deals with the first six before moving on. It will draw a first conclusion, to which it will give the most weight. It will only handle the other information after that. Showing only six figures to a decision maker to provide a first global overview of a situation is one of the best-established rules of cognitive ergonomics (see Montague, 2006; Pinker, 1999).

Another lesson from cognitive sciences was developed for airline pilots' decision making. Their basic instrument panel has six dials, which answer pilots' six basic questions: Am I safe in the short and the long term? What are my short- and long-term resource levels? Where am I headed in the short and the long term? The speed and altitude indicators are the primary sources of safety for airline pilots. Attitude and trim indicators show their resources for manoeuvre. Position and track visuals indicate their goals.

The same questions implicitly arise in the frontal lobes of the manager's brain. The SFM method facilitates this approach to decision making:

1 The question 'Am I safe now?' is answered by measurement of time facing customers. If managers lose contact with their market, they will quickly face danger.

2 The question 'Am I safe in the long term?' is answered by measurement of sales from new sources, which shows the ability to adapt.

3 The question 'What are my resource levels in the short term?' is answered by measurement of gains from processes, which shows the ability to quickly reposition resources from one activity to another.

4 The question 'What is the level of my long-term resources?' is answered by measurement of the people responsibility level, which shows the ability to use human resources to best effect.

5 The question 'Will I achieve my short-term goals?' is answered by measurement of return on critical resource, which shows the ability to optimally use what is available.

6 The question 'Will I achieve my long-term goals?' is answered by measurement of key project status, which shows the ability to improve things rapidly.

Aircraft pilots also rely on a variant of six figure management to reach their objectives. Instructors teach trainee pilots to display six figures for most aircraft moves. These can be related to business indicators:

Business indicator panel	Aircraft indicator panel
Sales from new sources (SFN)	Climb rate indicator
Time facing customers (TFC)	Heading indicator
Gains from processes (GFP)	Power indicator
People responsibility level (PRL)	Attitude indicator
Return on critical resource (RCR)	Speed indicator
Key project status (KPS)	Turn coordination indicator

The sales from new sources measure is the 'climb rate indicator'

In aviation, altitude means security. Flying upwards is transforming resources (fuel) into altitude. Gaining altitude means going far and being safe. Being high in the air is the guarantee for having a vantage viewpoint.

It's the same thing in business. Investing in new activities keeps you safe in surveillance mode.

The time facing customers measure is the 'heading indicator'

Direction is crucial in aviation. It's where you're heading. Pilots are given direction with the help of satellites. The better the reception, the more precise the pilot is.

In business, direction is given by the customer and the market. The more you know, the more precise your direction towards your goals will be.

The gains from processes measure is the 'power indicator'

In aviation, power enables many things: going up, changing direction fast, and getting there before the others do. This power is the result of the energy that your engine produces by burning fuel.

In business it's the same. It's about burning organizational energy to produce value and innovation ahead of the competition. Processes are the equivalent of the aeroplane's engine.

The people responsibility level measure is the 'attitude indicator'

In aviation, an aeroplane's attitude is its position in space. Oriented upwards or downwards and tilted to one side or the other, the attitude translates speed into movement in space.

In business, the attitude is your position towards employees, and it's an investment that translates into results and change.

The return on critical resource measure is the 'speed indicator'

In aviation, speed is a result of the aeroplane's most critical resource, its fuel.

In business, your fuel is the investment you make. Investment in both capital and employee motivation is crucial.

The key project status measure is the 'turn coordination indicator'

In aviation, the turn coordination indicator helps the pilot fine-tune turns without deviating.

In business, the key project status measure enables entrepreneurs to turn their businesses around without deviating from the target.

Pilots are constantly trained in doing six figure management

Aviation pilots are trained to follow their own six figures in the cockpit in order to guide them through their flight. Especially in times of stress, crisis and problems, they have to constantly go back to the fundamentals. In modern aircraft, there are three altimeters that give the same information, as this information is critical for the pilots.

The three questions that the pilot/manager should be able answer quickly, at all times, are:

1 Are we safe?

- In the short term: read the answer on your heading indicator/time facing customers indicator.
- In the long term: read the answer on your climb rate indicator/sales from new sources indicator.

2 Do we have enough resources?

- In the short term: read the answer on your power indicator/gains from processes indicator.
- In the long term: read the answer on your altitude indicator/people responsibility level indicator.

3 Are we heading where we plan to go? Will we reach our objectives?

- In the short term: read the answer on your speed indicator/return on critical resource indicator.
- In the long term: read the answer on your turn coordination indicator/key project status indicator.

Human intelligence is a fairly simple system once you break it down to basics. The brain sets objectives and then transforms these objectives into actions with minimum effort and means (see Figure 1.1). The brain also transforms information into knowledge by using intellectual and personal processes. All of this is done to deliver one movement.

FIGURE 1.1 The manager's intelligence: three steps, six measures

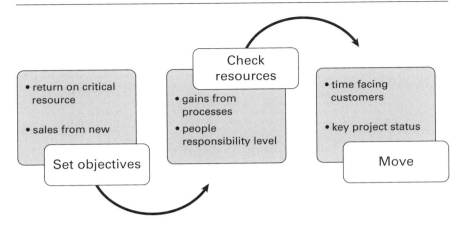

FIGURE 1.2 The manager's thinking process

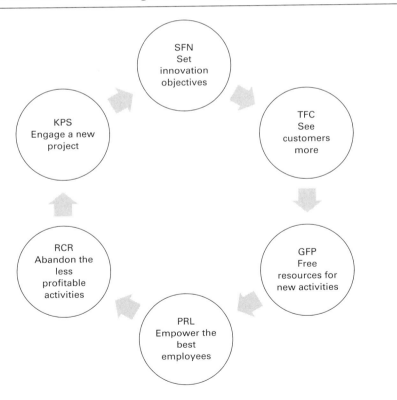

Into the executive brain

Step 1

I should move, change and innovate to survive and thrive. I will set this objective and monitor this move with sales from new sources.

Step 2

Who will give me the best advice on moving along in the right direction? Obviously, it will be my environment, market, customers and competitors. I will thus increase my time facing customers.

Step 3

From where will my resources come to permit that move? They will come safely from freeing resources through gains from doing things in a more elegant and economical way. I will thus monitor my gains from processes performance.

Step 4

To whom should I delegate those resources to make that move happen? Obviously, it will be to those with a track record of success. I will thus measure our people responsibility level indices.

Step 5

This move should be oriented towards economic and social results. Our return on critical resource should thus be on display on our dashboard.

Step 6

To make this move happen, I will manage it as a structured project and display the status of this project at the front of my desk.

Innovation reverse engineering

Set innovation objectives

If you want to gather good ideas for innovation, then increase your customer closeness and organize more frequent customer contacts.

See customers more

If you want more customer focus, then free resources by processing production activities better.

Free resources for new activities

If you want to improve your processes quickly, then give more responsibilities to your best people and do it fast.

Empower the best employees

If you want to hire the best people, then improve the profitability of your business by abandoning low-added-value activities.

Abandon the less profitable activities

If you want to identify and abandon your low-profitability activities, design and focus on only one key change project.

Why you can rely on the SFM method

The SFM method is based on the study of hundreds of companies. Its experience-based nature, resulting from the in-depth analysis of numerous business cases, makes it effective in delivering the business results it promises.

Summary

You know how the SFM method works, on what research background it is based and how managers use it.

What's next

In the next chapter we will review how to integrate the SFM method into your current management methods and leadership.

How SFM will help you to get the most from your reporting systems

02

KEY LEARNING POINTS

- The six figure management method provides a proved content for reporting frameworks.

- It improves the efficiency of your performance management tools and your balanced scorecards.

- It provides a reporting framework to balance the key performance indicators amongst four perspectives and your Management Cockpits.

- It is a piloting framework to present information in a way that facilitates team decisions and actions.

The evolution of business performance measurement

Business performance measurement (BPM) first appeared in the 19th century with the birth of financial accounting. This was followed by the second generation in the 20th century: balancing financial indicators with non-financial measurement such as activities, volumes of sales and production, customer satisfaction, employee satisfaction, process results, quality and productivity, and market shares. The balanced scorecard was born in this context.

The third generation from the 21st century meant adding business intelligence, cognitive ergonomics, models, content and benchmarks to the previous generation. It saw the birth of big data, the Management Cockpit (MC) and the six figure management (SFM) method.

The balanced scorecard, a major advance in business performance management

What is the balanced scorecard?

The balanced scorecard (BSC) is a famous consulting method promoted by management consultant David P Norton and accounting professor Robert S Kaplan at the end of the 20th century (see Kaplan and Norton, 1996). The BSC is a dash-board method recommending the balancing of performance measurements between the four classical sectors: finance-related performance, commerce-related performance, process-related performance and strategy-related performance.

It claims a background of a one-year survey with 12 companies in the original article. The notion of balance between perspectives is essential for this method. Its main recommendation is to divide the presentation of business performance measurements into four blocks: financial, commercial, internal and innovation.

Even though the BSC is a very efficient management tool, it has its deficiencies. SFM is designed to address these deficiencies but also to keep the advantages of the BSC. Designed to address the very top level of the organization, the BSC addresses more abstract and less actionable aspects of the company. It does not address down-to-earth operational aspects. The SFM is designed to deal with both high-level and operational-level issues.

The BSC presents itself to executives as a nice but empty box. Thanks to its pragmatic, more universal level of implementation, the SFM is a true Swiss-army knife, highly adaptable and capable of addressing most current business situations. Less strategic guessing is necessary beforehand; fewer action drivers are necessary after. It's simple and straightforward without being simplistic and arrogant.

The BSC handles strategic perspectives at a global level:

- finance;
- commercial;
- processes;
- growth.

The SFM anchors the BSC at a real business-life level, with more focused performance and with employees foregrounded:

- sales from new sources (SFN);
- time facing customers (TFC);

- gains from processes (GFP);
- people responsibility level (PRL);
- return on critical resource (RCR);
- key project status (KPS).

To summarize, the main difference is the bottom-up approach of the SFM compared to the top-down approach of the BSC.

Practice and time have shown that many BSC projects launched by companies didn't survive. They were often imposed by upper management and probably lacked simplicity and employee commitment. The six KPIs of the SFM method are designed to motivate all personnel:

1 to innovate thanks to the measurement and display of their SFN performance;

2 to spend more time with customers, thanks to the measurement and display of their TFC performance;

3 to reduce costs and time delays, thanks to the measurement and display of their GFP performance;

4 to trust the best people more, thanks to the measurement and display of their PRL performance;

5 to optimize rare resources, thanks to the measurement and display of their RCR performance;

6 to focus on one major change project at a time, thanks to the measurement and display of their KPS performance.

SFM is an evolution beyond the balanced scorecard

In order to ensure a fair survival rate for the method in companies, the SFM programme has drawn lessons from the application of the BSC in the field. It adds human and leadership perspectives to the BSC and distances itself from strategic, financial and accounting perspectives.

We call the programme the 'six figure management method' and not the 'six figure scorecard' because of its human and operational aspects:

1 *The evolution toward simplicity.* The SFM concept provides only six KPIs to be measured from the outset. They are considered to be the essential and universal measurements for any company that wants to prosper.

2 *The evolution to becoming highly operational.* The most operational level of SFM compared to the BSC is closer to employees and more motivating. Employees are not motivated by the free cash flow that often appears in the BSC.

3 *The evolution toward personnel.* The SFM method adds two human dimensions to the four BSC perspectives: personal accountability, with the PRL performance measurements; and leadership, with the KPS performance measurements.

4 *The evolution to decentralization.* The SFM is built from the bottom up in an organization, contrary to the BSC, which cascades from top to bottom in the organization. The SFM is decentralized. The operational units build their dashboards first. They are then consolidated toward the top. The market is the basis for this strategy; managers in the field know it well. The field dashboards are, therefore, often naturally in line with the organization's strategy.

5 *The evolution to action.* The six SFM KPIs are merely the visible tip of the approach. The SFM method provides key business rules for each of them, promoting their

improvement. Examples of business rules geared to improving those six key performance areas are presented in the Conclusion. The message of the SFM method is one of process:

- Try more new things.
- Spend more time with customers.
- Do the same things with fewer costs and delays.
- Give more to the best people.
- Invest more in your most critical resource.
- Focus on one big change project only.

FIGURE 2.1   SFM, a bottom-up complement to the BSC approach

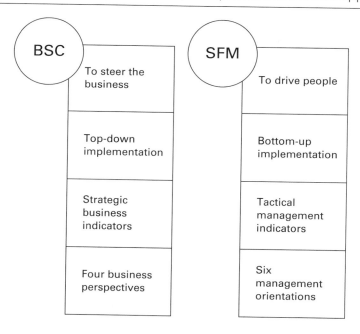

The Management Cockpit, another advance in dashboards

After reviewing a second-generation performance management framework, the balanced scorecard, we will now examine a third-generation performance management tool, the Management Cockpit (see Georges and Sinzig, 2000; Georges, 2004), which, as we shall see, will drive us to SFM.

What's a Management Cockpit?

A Management Cockpit (MC), as described in the Introduction, is a performance management tool that has been on the market for more than 10 years. It looks like an aircraft cockpit. Executives call it a war room for business cases. Its major advantage is its ergonomics. The MC is a 'decision support system' type of dashboard system. It presents the KPIs of the piloted organization in a very actionable way, on four walls, physical or virtual, titled respectively: Will we reach our objectives? What are the levels of our resources? What are the obstacles that we face? Are we acting/moving/changing according to our plans?

It was developed in Europe and first described by one of the authors, Patrick M Georges, who later partnered with Grégoire Talbot, a manager at IBM, to develop the system.

Note: Management Cockpit® is a trademark of the company Cockpit Group.

What's a Management Cockpit question?

The contribution of the MC approach resides essentially in its scientific advances in decision-making support. Based on solid studies in decision and cognitive sciences, it makes the presentation of information more intuitive to decision makers and easier to understand by managers.

For example, the presentation of the KPIs is done in a question-and-answer format. The questions most frequently asked by managers when making business decisions are answered with a few performance indicators. Many studies demonstrate that this way of presenting information facilitates decision making.

Typical questions answered by KPIs, comments, facts and figures on the MC panels are:

- Are we satisfying our customers?
- Are we increasing our quality and productivity?
- Are we reducing our costs and delays?
- Are we increasing our sales activities?

What's a Management Cockpit visual cascade?

Other advances in cognitive ergonomics have been integrated to provide better visualization of business situations. The visual cascade consists of four layers for each KPI: a table of figures, a traffic light, graphics, and a decision support visual. The amount of information and size of the visuals vary depending on their significance and critical situation. This facilitates information analysis by decision makers. The details and causal factors of the KPIs are shown, or not shown, to the manager depending on the KPI values and targets. If the KPI is in the green zone, the causal factors will not be automatically displayed.

What's a Management Cockpit wall, physical or virtual?

Scientists define human intelligence as the ability to achieve the highest objectives, when faced with obstacles, using a minimum amount of resources, and with rapid action. In an MC, decision information is presented in four groups, on four walls: the black wall, with 'Will we achieve our objectives?'; the red wall, with 'What obstacles do we have to overcome (the market)?'; the blue wall, with 'Do we have the necessary resources (the processes)?'; and the white wall, with 'Do we adjust quickly enough (the projects)?' This grouping on four walls was decided based on the results of recent research in cognitive sciences that demonstrated that it is the right sequence for presenting information to the human mind to help ensure that correct decisions are taken.

How the SFM method works together with the Management Cockpit approach

One of the tricky steps during the implementation of an MC is the selection of the right indicators. The SFM method helps here by providing universal KPIs that should be part of many dashboards but that are flexible enough to be easily adapted to all industrial sectors and strategies.

In a way, the SFM provides the leading content, while the MC complements it with structure and causal factors. The SFM refocuses managers on a very few numbers of MC indicators, forcing them to apply the 'First things first' rule in business.

Now that we've reviewed the method, it's time to discuss individual performance. 'Mark' will be our guide, and will feature in the following chapters.

The SFM model is beneficial at the level of the individual manager, as well as at the level of the organization. The manager is seen as a 'one-person business'. As a sort of CEO of his or her own organization, the manager can use the six KPIs of the SFM to become more organized, more focused and more productive. We use the example of Mark, a typical manager working in a typical organization, at the beginning of each chapter, to illustrate, in its simplest form, how each of the KPIs can be applied. Mark is the manager of a small team of people, has been working for a couple of years in the same company and is facing various problems. These are issues that all managers face or should consider in order to be efficient. Luckily, his friend John is there for support and clarification. John has been a manager for much longer than Mark and he acts like a professional coach to Mark, sharing his wisdom and experience whenever the situation calls for it.

Summary

You now know how to benefit globally from the SFM method.

What's next

In the next chapter, we will review the first step of your growing strategy: measuring and improving innovation.

Try more new things

Measuring and improving your sales from new sources performance

---

03

KEY LEARNING POINTS

- You will learn how to improve innovation in your organization effectively and quickly.

- You will be able to choose the best sales from new sources indicator to measure in your particular situation.

- You will learn how to improve your sales from new sources once you've started measuring them.

This is the story of Mark, a young manager from a typical company; let's call it Every Business. His more experienced friend John is his mentor and guides him through times of trouble. Let's discover how Mark decided to apply sales from new sources in order to solve his professional issues.

Mark was feeling excluded and neglected. After five years on the job, he found that his colleagues were not asking for his expertise any more and he was left out of meetings. He decided to talk to John.

John thought about it for a moment and then asked him the following questions: 'Did you try to expand your network inside the organization?' Have you recently tried to add to your expertise?' 'What are the means by which you market yourself inside the organization?'

Mark had to face the facts. In the past few years he had not evolved professionally in any way. He did not offer anything new in terms of expertise, and his visibility in the organization was extremely low. He was content to do what he had always been doing and nothing more.

Mark pulled himself together. It was time to take the initiative to solve his problem. By undertaking a training programme in project management he further developed and enriched his expertise. Through an internal web page, he marketed his newly acquired skills to his colleagues.

In a short time, he was back on track. He was invited to take part in numerous projects and meetings. His boss congratulated him on his comeback and offered him an increase in his responsibilities as well as an additional budget for new ventures.

Mark thought it was a good idea to apply and scale this method to his team and, moreover, to his organization. He came up with a proposition to implement 'sales from new sources' as an organization objective, following the outcome of his personal success story. This covered:

- revenues from new products;
- cash from new customers;
- budgets from new sources;
- sales from new partners;
- profits from new distribution channels;
- incomes from new competencies;
- means generated by new activities.

Sales from new sources (SFN) measures your organization's capacity for innovation. You need to measure and improve your innovation in order to progress. Keeping track of this will motivate you to launch new activities.

What does the term *sales* stand for? It's up to you to decide. Do not narrow-mindedly fixate yourself on the word *sales*. According to your own activity, replace *sales* with *orders*, *revenue*, *budget*, *production*, *activity*, *means* or *profits*. The method is the same.

What is *new*? It's up to you to decide, depending on your sector of activity. If you are working in the IT sector, activities that have occurred in the past one or two years can be considered as *new*. If you are in the heavy industry sector, *new* is what you weren't doing five years ago. The value of *new* follows the pace of the industry from which you come.

Whatever you choose this indicator to be, the SFN will measure innovation in your organization. The higher the value of your SFN, the higher your profit margins will be, the more market share you will earn, and the more the satisfaction of your clients will increase. It is mere common sense.

Sales from new sources in action

To explore further the type of situation Mark and many managers in a similar position find themselves in, we will look at the example of a large high-tech company that wants to boost its level of innovation and has simply measured the percentage of sales attributable to its old products (more than five years old): 76 per cent. The measurement has been benchmarked against those of its two main competitors, which measured 62 and 46 per cent. The message is clear for everyone: the competitors are bringing forward more successful new products and have a competitive advantage. However, an innovation campaign by itself will be useless if the outcome is not measured. SFN is an easy and straightforward way of measuring the level of innovation within an organization. As the brief scenarios below demonstrate, SFN can be applied and customized in many different ways in order to reflect the needs of the manager or business.

They asked themselves a tricky question: SFN for what?

A service company that implemented the SFM method questioned whether to implement the SFN of their own services or that of their client. Their success was defined by how much their client was being innovative. Before deciding to implement the SFM method, they never asked themselves this type of question.

They didn't even know their SFN before

We asked an entrepreneur a simple and basic question about his company: has your company's sales proposition of new products been improving or not over the past few years? He was puzzled and did not know what answer to give, not even by looking through his company database and KPIs.

They selected a very particular SFN

One particular user of our methodology decided to choose sales from new suppliers as his innovation indicator. He explained to us that, in his line of business, it is highly critical to renew his supplier in order to take advantage of new innovation sources and opportunities.

They want to be the best in class on one point

A large public service that has been using the SFM method fixed a clear objective: that its sales from new technology – a high-speed drill technology, which was 31 per cent in the past year – should double within a year.

They want to increase sales

A company chose sales from new salespeople as its indicator, aware of the fact that, after four years, revenue per salesperson usually stagnated. It is thus important to maintain a proportion above 20 per cent of revenues coming from staff who have been in the company for less than two years.

They are in the public sector and need to choose a KPI

For institutions like museums and hospitals, the proportion of new sources of revenue has become increasingly important because of the decrease in the usual sources of public financing. These revenues may come from sponsors, new client segments and so on. Most hospitals target an increase in new revenue sources of 30 per cent. The KPI that hospital groups use to describe this is 'new revenues from non-public sources'.

They want to compare themselves to the best

Data providers are amassing more and more information concerning companies, and selling this information to market analysts, consultants or even directly to companies that are interested in understanding their competitors' performance. If you want to find out what the SFN of your main competitor is, these companies will sell you the intelligence that they have obtained by putting together in-depth analysis of basic information. If you don't actually sell anything, open your mind; you can still use the same indicator (see Figure 3.1). What is the equivalent of 'sales' for you: orders, means, budgets, incomes, internal sales?

FIGURE 3.1   Selecting the right SFN for your business situation

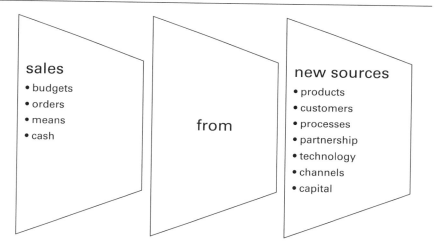

sales
- budgets
- orders
- means
- cash

from

new sources
- products
- customers
- processes
- partnership
- technology
- channels
- capital

Who should measure and improve SFN performance?

1 *You as a professional.* What new competencies have you recently been using? How many people in the organization have you shared your recently acquired

expertise with? Examples at your level include returns from new competencies and benefits from new contacts.

2 *Your team or your unit.* How many of your unit's new services have other units, your internal customers, recently ordered? Your SFN will be internal demand for new services.

3 *Your organization, whether it is publicly or privately held.* What new products have you developed and sold recently? How many new clients have you targeted and acquired lately?

The focus of this chapter is on managers implementing SFN on an organizational level, but feel free to extrapolate to yourself or to your team.

Why should managers measure their SFN performance?

Innovation is a key metric for any organization, because it enables it to follow the fast trends of today's dynamic environment. Many managers look at innovation as a key component of their business, but how many of them actually measure and manage innovation? Not nearly enough!

When it comes to innovation, managers do not possess appropriate measurement tools. The challenge is that innovation is viewed as an abstract notion, and managers find innovation difficult to quantify (see Hadedoom and Cloodt, 2003; Smith, 2005; Walker, Jeannes and Rowlands, 2002).

A lot of managers make the common mistake of considering all new organization activities as innovation, when innovation should refer only to the success rate of new activities. This can generate a misleading appreciation of the level of innovation in your organization, leading to overestimation and consequently underperformance.

As soon as you define a clear, pragmatic way to measure the level of innovation, it becomes an easy-to-use metric in your organization. If you are able to measure your level of innovation, you can start managing innovation in your organization.

SFN is easy to implement and, once put in place, it conveys the following advantages:

- innovation is now a realistic measurement of your organization's performance;
- your organization is managing its innovation level and can align its strategy accordingly;
- managers and employees across your organization are motivated to embrace innovation broadly and give it ongoing priority;
- innovation is no longer mistaken for the pursuit of new activities, which can be both successful and unsuccessful;
- new activities that are not successful can be identified and discarded, avoiding the waste of resources.

A high value for the SFN might mean a high level of:

- new product development (eg a large percentage of revenue generated from new products);
- continuous improvement (eg products are becoming better and better, resulting in quality leadership on the market);
- technological leadership (eg first in class in number of patents per year);
- product diversification (eg serving the widest range of customer profiles on the market).

A low value for the SFN might mean:

- not enough incentives for developing new activities (eg no bonuses based on innovation);
- low success rates for new initiatives (eg no profit for newly launched products).

How do you implement the SFN measurements and improvements?

The implementation of SFN is easy once you answer the following three questions related to your business:

- What is the name for *sales* in my organization? Choose between income, orders, means, budget, sales and so on.
- Sales from new what? Choose an indicator from the examples below. Select the ones that are appropriate for measuring the SFN of your organization.
- What are the benchmarks?

Apply these indicators wisely, in order to position your SFN value to the level that you are strategically targeting.

Sales from new what?

Establish your own customized definition for SFN depending on your business. SFN may refer to the percentage of sales generated by new products, services, clients, distribution channels, locations, etc. It may refer to anything that affects sales and is representative of your business. For example, a restaurant may establish an SFN from new products, which would mean seasonally different items on the menu.

What are the indicators that best measure SFN performance?

Choose your SFN from those discussed below, which are the most popular performance indicators. If your strategy is clear, then it will indicate what the most appropriate SFNs are for your organization.

Sales from new products or services

This is the most straightforward way to measure your SFN. It may refer to this year's additional budget for new ventures, the earnings due to new products or services, the new resources that result from an improvement in your services, etc.

Testimonial: An operation engineer at a fine chemical plant

'Our three main competitors are achieving 10 per cent of their revenues from new products. This is what our consultants have told us. Because innovation is a big part of our business, we have fixed a target SFN at 12 per cent. In order to achieve this target, we count on the suggestions that our research department will provide.'

Sales from new clients, external or internal

Do not limit yourself to the terms 'sales' and 'clients'. Think broadly about what these might represent with regard to your own business.

Testimonial: A marketing manager at a US express delivery company

'Our objective is to achieve 8 per cent of our clients from outside the usual customer catchment area. We have delegated two of our best sales representatives for this task.'

Testimonials: Managers at an internal support unit

'The functional requirements that my team needs to fulfil are well defined within the organization. I cannot create new functions for my team. However, for us, the SFN is represented by new internal clients of the organization that start using what we deliver, people that have not been using our services in previous years. These are new internal clients for the existing services.'

'In order to improve our SFN performance, we have initiated a page on our organization's intranet to better market our competencies throughout the organization, across different countries and different departments. We have been surprised by the number of new requests for services. Because of the shift in workload, our team has been granted additional resources!'

Sales from new activities

These are the means and the advantages that result from new activities. You can measure this as the revenues generated from the time and personnel allocated to new activities. Through this indicator you simply measure the number of people or working hours allocated to activities that have occurred recently.

'Every quarter, my team receives the objective of providing a new service to our organization. Most of the time this consists of a mere improvement to the current service that we provide internally.'

'Each year, I establish a personal target that I care deeply about. It's not part of my job description, but it's my baby, and if it's successful I am definitely going to make a name for myself in the organization!'

'Every year, I book a day with my team to discuss the following questions. Which are the competencies and expertise that are underused or unknown even within our own organization? How can we reinforce these competencies? How can we better market ourselves internally?'

Sales from new distribution channels

These are the additional resources, financial or otherwise, that you achieve as a result of addressing your market through new channels: newly opened sites, a new partnership network, new virtual channels, etc.

Testimonial: An executive in charge of business development in a retail business

'Our objective is to have 5 per cent of sales coming from our new website. In all our stores, our sales personnel inform clients about the advantages of buying online: you save time by ordering from home or from your office, and on top of that you get a 5 per cent discount!'

Sales from new suppliers

Your suppliers are as important to your business as your clients are. They can help develop innovation and can even contribute to enlarging your distribution channels within the regions that they serve.

Testimonial: A purchase manager

'We conduct a retail business. We buy and then resell with a margin. It is important for us to ask our suppliers for innovative products and constantly look for new suppliers. All this is conducted in order to improve our SFN.'

Sales from new partnerships

New partnerships are meant to open doors to different activities and regions, and can allow your organization to capture a different set of clients and venture into innovative projects together. This is a great way of sharing knowledge, and can lead to an increase in efficiency.

Testimonial: A board member at an airline company

'We improve our SFN performance by constantly seeking new partnerships. We then calculate the percentage of revenue that has been generated as a result of these collaborations.'

Sales from new technologies

If you've recently introduced a new technology in production or sales, calculate the proportion of revenues generated by using this new technology in comparison to the revenues corresponding to former technologies.

Testimonial: A computer scientist at a manufacturing company

'On our scoreboard, we have a clear target. By the end of the year we should produce 75 per cent of our product C with the new technology A.'

Sales from budget allocations for innovative ventures

Organizations want to implement projects that bring change and progress. The amount of resources allocated to these types of projects can be a candidate for your SFN indicator.

Testimonial: A board member at a large software company

'We do not believe in creating innovation internally. We are always on the lookout for small innovative start-ups that have a clear record of satisfied clients and that seek to grow but do not have the means to do so. We offer them financial support and benefits from our economies of scale. We use them as research cells, far more dynamic and less costly than any internal research department.'

Other indicators that you may consider to appraise your SFN performance

The lead time between the occurrence and the implementation of a new idea

Although not as straightforward as other indicators, this can also be a measure of your SFN. You compare the time dedicated to initiate a project to the corresponding outcome in terms of sales once the project has been implemented.

The budget allocated for R&D

This is the percentage of sales due to a team or a person in charge of researching new activities within your organization. The R&D of an organization is usually not linked to sales, because the return on this effort is not directly reflected in revenues. However, the indirect value of R&D in an organization is high, because it relates to a future investment.

Sales from new patents

This is the revenue resulting from selling or licensing patent-holding products or services. It usually applies to a particular business model and is especially important for high-tech organizations.

Sales from new locations or points of sale

Expanding your geographical presence will earn you market share and a new pool of clients. A positive side effect is the diversification of products and services that need to be customized to local needs. This will be an indicator for both innovation and growth in your organization.

The cost of abandoned projects

You will participate in many activities and initiate a great deal of innovative projects, but not all of them will be successful. The success rate of new projects is generally low. Consequently, you will be forced to cut budgets and cease activities for those projects that have failed.

Calculate the budget that has been invested in these wasted trials. If this represents more than a couple of percentage points of your revenue, you are too creative and too open to try out new things. If the percentage is close to zero, then you are not daring enough, you do not take enough risk and you are not trying to adapt to external changes. Find the right balance between the two.

There are numerous ways of evaluating your will to change, as well as the innovation and progress in your organization. It's up to you to come up with indicators that are most suited for your business, starting from the examples mentioned.

What are the benchmarks?

Clear benchmark values for the SFN must also be established by the organization. It is essential for the SFN to reflect tangible results that can be interpreted with respect to these benchmarks, because strategic decisions are to be taken based on these results. Compare your SFN with your own past performance, with comparable best-in-class organizations and with data provided by market information vendors.

How do you effectively use SFN performance?

The SFN is an easy-to-implement, easy-to-use tool that will provide a good and realistic indicator for innovation in your organization because it quantifies the success factor of new activities based on tangible results.

Once you put the SFN in place in your organization, communicate the results to the organization on a quarterly basis and align your innovation strategy to these results. It's as easy as that. For example, if the average percentage of sales from the new item for the entire year is below an expected threshold, the strategic decision is to cancel the product.

Independent of the positive or negative outlook of the quarterly results, you need to align your strategy by pursuing a detailed analysis of the SFN. Based on the value of your SFN, ask yourself the following questions:

- what are the activities, clients and services that we didn't have one year ago?
- what percentage of my organization's resources is currently allocated to these new projects?
- what is the success rate of these new projects?
- is this value growing or diminishing?
- is this value higher or lower than the average industry figures?
- what is the proportion of the organization's resources allocated to new unique activities, compared to those resources allocated to recurrent process-driven activities?
- how much cash, time and personnel in my organization are allocated for research into new activities?

- how did organizations like mine manage to increase their market share?
- how many on-site visits to organizations that are innovative do we organize per year?
- how can my organization continue to improve and create value in the future?
- where are the areas in which my organization may grow through innovation?

How can managers improve a bad SFN performance?

You have defined two or three appropriate SFN indicators for your business. You have accurately measured them. Now you should improve these values. What are the most popular methods that managers use for improving the SFN?

Open innovation

The chief marketing officer of SAP AG said:

> Our clients, our suppliers and our employees make up our research department on innovation. We follow a well-developed process to collect and reward new ideas and potential improvements to our products. A supplier feels it a great privilege to contribute an innovative idea to our business. A client who gives us an idea for a new product and tests the prototype will get a discount for all future purchases. Any employee who directly contributes in achieving one pound of profit or in saving one hour of our time will receive significant benefits.

Compare yourself to an organization that you consider innovative

Choose an innovative organization that isn't a competitor. Meet the management. Ask them to share their SFN indicator values with you.

Incentivize your sales force to promote your new products and reach for new customers

Organize promotional campaigns for new products. Offer your sales personnel incentives to concentrate on new products rather than on old ones. Be careful not to cannibalize your business through the success of new products.

Set individual commissioning based on the percentage of new clients that have been successfully reached from the targeted population of potential clients.

Invest in R&D

Name a person to be responsible for changes and progress in your organization. This person should incentivize employees, customers and suppliers to come up with new ideas, research the literature for potential improvements for the organization, keep watch over the newest trends in technology, etc. The basic way to incentivize people is to offer compensation for concrete deliverables. A lot of companies practise giving out bonuses per patent. Others reward entire R&D teams based on the success of the product. A percentage of the profit can be included in the variable salary of these R&D employees. Too often marketing alone takes credit for the success of years of research by the engineering department. Even though the revenues are not directly linked to their activity, a token of appreciation and recognition can boost motivation in R&D. Other types of incentives are related to responsibilities. Compensating a research engineer by giving him or her team responsibility may work as an innovation booster for some. Make sure you know what motivates your employees before you jump into deciding on incentives.

Do not neglect your spending on equipment. If you have the latest tools, your team is equipped to deal with the latest trends and will get things done faster.

Buy licences, acquire organizations and form joint ventures

External growth is the perfect way to generate changes in the working environment, promote new ideas, gain new clients and develop new products.

Encourage employees, suppliers and clients to come up with new ideas

This can be implemented in the form of a think tank, as a compensation plan for the best green projects, as the sharing of organization benefits with the initiator, and so on.

Extend globally

Do not limit yourself to the borders of a country, a market or a well-known pool of clients. With the advancements in technology today, your potential market is growing and easier to target.

Take advantage of suppliers that may have a larger geographical reach than you, in order to expand your business. Today, it's easier to reach distant clients than it was five years ago.

Implement personal innovation project seminars

Invest thoroughly in your human resources: your organization's most important asset. Innovation is a result of people's creativity, so investment in personnel will indirectly increase your innovation.

Train your collaborators in how to reach for new ideas, and encourage them to think outside of the box.

You can count the number of personal innovation projects present within your organization. Personal innovation projects are the personal initiatives of employees that the organization endorses.

Establish alliances and partnerships with various stakeholders (clients, suppliers, the competition)

Techniques such as co-marketing, co-selling and co-production are nowadays classical methods used by organizations that want both to increase their innovation level and to be efficient. Being creative implies thinking outside of the box. How could you better achieve this than actually working with somebody from outside of the box? If you take a look at co-production, you will see the benefits immediately. The customer is involved in creating the product, cutting off production costs. The customer is actually undertaking part of the work, but most often this is viewed as an increase in the flexibility of a valuable experience. The customer is sometimes willing to pay more to get this type of product. A simple example is a cook-it-yourself restaurant. Customers pay a premium in order to enjoy the experience of cooking their own meal, while the establishment benefits from the cost reduction of not having to cook.

What are the limitations of measuring and improving your SFN performance?

A high-cost, high-risk game

Innovation is always risky. It can cost a lot in terms of time, personnel, cash, organization, direction, etc. Innovation is usually profitable, but not always.

Too many attempts can burn your cash too fast and stretch your business resources to the limit. Be sure you know your limitations when you push the innovation 'pedal to the metal'. The limit is usually related to the minimum amount of resources (usually cash) that you need in order for the company to survive. You stay within your limits by always predicting the outcome of an investment. The return on investment analysis should be correlated to the level of risk of the investment in order to get a realistic approach.

A sensitive issue

A large number of your collaborators may not embrace change. They can contribute to slowing down your initiatives because of their reluctance to change. It's up to you to convince and convert other people to become followers and embracers of change.

Cannibalization

Cannibalization is a phenomenon that results when a firm develops a new product or service that steals business or market share from its existing products and services. You have to be careful not to cannibalize your existing product and service offering, or at least make sure that it results in positive outcomes, higher profitability and gain in market share.

However, some innovative firms currently encourage the act of cannibalization and forced obsolescence. For example, when Coca-Cola introduced Diet Coke, a similar product, this took sales away from the original Coke, but ultimately led to an expanded market for diet soft drinks. By deliberately cannibalizing its major product, Coca-Cola managed to create a new innovative market.

Another example of cannibalization occurs when a retailer discounts a particular product. The tendency of consumers is to buy the discounted product rather than the normal full-sale version. This temporary change in consumer behaviour can be described as cannibalization.

CASE STUDY 3.1 An integrated approach to the SFM method

Breaking the silos for more innovation

A German insurance company was facing the difficult challenge of maintaining profitability and, as with most financial companies today, shareholders were asking for increased profits through better management processes. Its managers decided to boost innovation by measuring and improving four indicators measuring its SFN performance. To realize a better sales from new sources performance, it used the gains from processes (GFP) indicators to streamline its core business processes, freeing resources for new projects.

The company realized it needed a balanced scoreboard to help streamline the management process through the measurement and improvement of its GFP performance to free resources, through time facing customers (TFC) to grab new ideas from the market, and through the people responsibility level (PRL) to delegate those resources to its best people. In response, the company turned to the SFM method.

The company needed improved control within key areas of the organization like customer orientation and innovation, because these performance areas were split between different departments.

It took action by implementing a six figure scoreboard, with its adaptable approach to integrating units or measurement systems throughout an organization. 'Before we decided to go with the six figure method, we had a wide range of KPIs in place, and our goal was to provide guidance through actionable indicators more quickly and to enable faster action.' The main business driver behind the SFM project was to provide managers with a simple reporting framework.

Although other business performance measurement approaches were considered, the SFM was selected as the best choice for a single, integrated system. 'The key message is simplicity; that's what we bought.'

The company decided to rigorously standardize KPIs across the businesses using a single system. One by one, the six KPIs were implemented. 'We implemented the entire suite of six KPIs that exist within the SFM method.'

Gaining control at middle-management level

The insurance company was especially in need of KPI aggregation and simplification. 'We had perhaps more than 80 of them throughout the businesses. Our objective was to achieve a significant increase in KPI visibility across our group, and understand what drives us.'

The company applied the SFN first, before addressing any other performance area. Within a short time, the company realized clear advantages from the KPIs' deployment. 'The implementation provided people with an integrated KPI scoreboard for the first time.'

Empowering collaborators

The company next activated the PRL performance project to better manage the innovation process:

- 'In HR, we suffer from too slow people empowerment based on age and an average four-year job rotation.'

- 'Given the focus on middle-management control these days, we see the SFM project as the key enabler of profitable growth.'

- 'With the PRL project, the company took advantage of unified performance – compensation on merit, promotion policy, manager's evaluation, all integrated into one key performance area.'

Bottom line with the return on critical resource performance

Without a middle-management scoreboard for managing business units, the company lacked important controls. Innovation could not be followed, and customer orientation could not be triggered:

- 'Prior to the SFM project, we didn't have a company-wide KPI system, while leaving the choice of indicators that measure those performance areas to local managers.'

- 'We've implemented the SFM as the front end of our whole reporting system. I think the beauty of the SFM is its simplicity and adaptability.'

The implementation was divided into implementation phases. Phase one focused on SFN. The company implemented SFN products, customers and technology. Phase two was focused on GFP. Phase three was essentially focused on the PRL. The company continued to expand its use of the SFM to TFC, gaining ideas from customers to innovate. During the deployment, the SAP system acted as the data provider.

Summary

The first step is now over; you are going for innovation.

What's next

In the next chapter, we will review the second step of your growing strategy: measuring and improving customers' and competitors' closeness.

Spend more time with customers
Measuring and improving your time facing customers performance

We continue the story of Mark, the young manager from a typical company. His more experienced friend John is his coach and guides him through times of trouble. In this particular story, Mark has been leading a project for a couple of months. Everything seems to be going fine, but is he aligned with what the customer (his boss) really wants? Let's discover how Mark decided to apply the time facing customers indicator in order to solve his professional problems.

Mark had been noticing that his boss was not happy with him, despite the high quality of his work and services. Lately, the general attitude of his bosses and peers had been clearly reflecting a lack of interest towards both himself and his project. He decided to talk to John. John reflected for a moment and then asked him the following question: 'How much time do you spend in discussion with your boss during a working week?'

Mark felt that this question had nothing to do with his concerns. He bluntly answered that he generally spent very little time with his boss and that he did not intend to do anything about it, as he feared that losing focus from his actual work would be counter-productive. He further explained that any time spent on discussions would qualify as wasteful, because in front of the boss his sole purpose was to be productive and nothing more. John suggested that he should double the contact time with his boss and come back to see him in one month. He recalled that he himself had confronted a similar situation in his early manager days and that communication with his boss has helped him understand the underlying reasons for his dissatisfaction.

A month later, Mark came back to greet John with a big grin on his face. The quality of his relationship with his boss had significantly increased. The boss was now very satisfied with his work and had even shared with him the responsibility for an important new project. He had regained popularity among his peers. During a discussion over coffee, Mark had come to understand what his boss truly expected from him, which was very different from what he had believed. His boss was expecting more focus on the softer side of the project, typically that Mark should give more coaching to his team and develop a relationship with the other managers in order to cooperate better. Working hard day and night wouldn't get Mark anywhere, because it was the softer side of the project that needed mending. Mark therefore stopped over-delivering and started developing his team and relationship. This also meant fewer and more efficient working hours and more recognition from his superior. From there on, Mark decided never to neglect communication with his boss, his main customer in the company. He decided to measure and improve time spent with his boss, by using the number of meetings per week as a simple indicator.

Mark thought it was a good idea to apply and scale this simple method to the organization. Why couldn't managers measure the time spent facing customers to improve their business? The customers were the people they were serving, whether the boss, internal clients or external clients. Therefore he came up with a proposition to implement time facing customers as an organization objective, following the outcome of his personal success story.

What is time facing customers performance?

This can be:

- number of salespeople per market segment;
- salespeople hours per day in front of new customers;
- size of the facing surface with consumers;
- hours per week working with your boss or internal customers.

Is your business customer-oriented? Quantifying this orientation has often been explored (see Johnston, Brignall and Fitzgerald, 2002; Nykamp, 2001).

Time facing customers (TFC) measures your organization's customer focus. You need to measure and improve your customer focus in order to better understand and reach your customer. The closer the relationship with your customers, the more you are able to fulfil their needs. TFC basically evaluates the time that your organization spends in interacting with your customer.

What does the term *time* describe? It's up to you to decide, depending on your organization and activity. It may describe the time in minutes, hours or days that your sales force interacts with customers, but it can refer to the number of sales personnel, the surface of your window display, the number of magazine advertisements per month, the number of people attending events that you have sponsored, the number of visits to your organization's website, etc. You can categorize your time by the level of interaction with the customer, the quality of time (active or passive) and so on.

Whatever you choose this indicator to be, the TFC will measure customer focus. By increasing customer focus, your organization's offer will become a better fit to your customers' needs. The consequence will be an increase in sales and an increase in market share.

Time facing internal customers and time facing external customers

> ### Testimonial: A support unit manager
>
> 'I manage a business unit within a large corporation. My customers are other internal units. However, the TFC is as important for us as if we were dealing with external customers. It is mandatory to listen to our customers' needs. We consequently must spend more time with them. One contact per month is not enough. Prior to using TFC, we were not aware of the fact that our services were satisfying our customers less and less. This was simply because we did not see them often enough to really understand what was going on.'

It's amazing to notice the very different ways managers employ the TFC measurement discipline. In the following list of brief cases we want to show that managers have invented many different ways to use our TFC measurement recommendation to their own benefit.

An oil and gas company set as an annual objective that the sales force should spend more time with the client as opposed to spending it in the office. The company did not set any direct objectives in terms of volume of sales, because it knew that, if the TFC improved, so would sales.

A hotel chain decided to double the size of its reception desks in order to enable its clients to have quick access to the front-desk personnel. That way, clients would not hesitate to address the staff even regarding the smallest issue.

An IT company in the United States gave its employees smart-phones with an application that measured the time passed in front of customers.

The TFC of the sales force of a certain transport company improved 20 per cent over the previous year. Unfortunately, a more in-depth analysis showed that the salespeople were actually spending more time with unprofitable customers. The company consequently fine-tuned the TFC indicator to measure time spent in front of potential and profitable clients.

Fifty per cent of a company's sales personnel's time was spent facing the client. The company considered that there were no improvements to be made, that this was the maximum it could achieve. The only way to achieve the objective of having a TFC of 200 hours per week was to increase the number of salespeople.

An international telco measured its efficiency at serving clients. It did this in a very pragmatic way by measuring the average waiting time over the phone and answering delays for questions on the web.

A London bank decided to become more client-oriented. In its performance reports it added a category called 'Are we improving our TFC?', consisting of four improvement targets. These targets were: increase front-desk time facing the client by 10 per cent; increase the number of front-office people by 10 per cent; decrease the amount of time spent responding to client questions by 10 per cent; and increase agency opening hours by 10 per cent.

If 'time spent' is not the relevant metric to appraise the effectiveness of your interface with your market, just open your mind and select another one, eg the size of the surface where you can interact with the customer, the number of available salespeople, or answer delays by your call centre (see Figure 4.1). Segment your customers to increase the relevance of this indicator.

FIGURE 4.1   Selecting the right TFC for your business situation

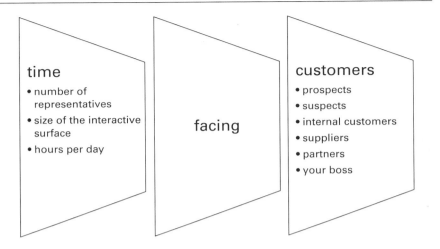

To whom does the TFC indicator apply?

1 *To you as a professional individual.* What activities have you initiated lately for the purpose of better understanding the needs and interests of your internal 'customers': your subordinates, your colleagues and your boss? How often do you request feedback from them? How do you use their feedback to better mould your activity to the real needs of the organization?

2 *To your team or unit.* Do you know exactly who your clients are within the organization? Do you clearly understand their needs?

3 *To your organization, whether it is publicly or privately held.* Does your customer come first? What are the methods you use in order to give your customer the highest priority?

The focus of this chapter is on managers implementing TFC on an organizational level, but feel free to extrapolate to your own personal scoreboard level or to your team scoreboard.

> Testimonial: A first-line manager at a Swiss consumer goods company
>
> 'I have three customers: my boss, the finance manager and the boss of my boss. This year, I've managed to increase my individual TFC toward them by 30 per cent. The effects have been quickly visible within my business unit: an increase in budget and far more autonomy.'

Why should managers measure their TFC performance?

> Testimonial: A middle manager from the commercial department of a US pharmaceutical company
>
> 'For us, reporting the TFC of our teams is mandatory and needs to be highly detailed. This is simply because our experience tells us that the higher our TFC, the more we sell.'

Managers today often measure and analyse their organization's performance by looking at abstract figures such as free cash flow or EBIT. Managers need to measure the actionable cause of the results instead of abstract financials that are merely the late results of these issues. Few people are motivated by free cash flow! Managers need indicators that motivate them to take action.

TFC is a figure that can explain the cause of your organization's current performance. This is because, whatever your business is, your success is going to depend on the relationship that you have with the customer.

TFC is something that everyone in the organization can relate to and that is meaningful and motivating. As soon as you are able to measure your customer focus, you can start managing it.

TFC is motivating and easy to implement and can offer the following advantages:

- customer focus is now a realistic measurement of your organization's performance and not just a concept that nobody really follows;
- your organization can compare itself to other organizations in terms of customer focus;
- everyone throughout your organization is motivated to prioritize on customer focus;
- the organization–customer relationship is now fully controlled by you, and improvement in this area will directly increase sales and market share.

A high value for the TFC might mean a high level of:

- customer loyalty;
- positive word of mouth that attracts more customers;
- efficiency of the sales force department of your organization;
- knowledge about the needs and expectations of your customers.

A low value for the TFC might mean:

- high customer turnover or a low customer retention rate;
- loss of market share to organizations that have a better knowledge of the customer;

- low efficiency of your business because your efforts are not focused on customer needs.

How do you implement the measurement and improvement of your TFC performance?

There are a multitude of ways to define and implement your TFC. It's up to you to decide what suits you best based on your area of business, your current activities, your budget, the values that you already measure and report, or the facility of measuring new values.

Do not forget to benchmark these values to those of competitors or to establish clear thresholds in order to perform an accurate analysis.

There are six easy steps to follow if you want to implement TFC:

1 decide if your organization values the commercial aspect of your activities and if customer focus is of high priority;

2 choose the TFC indicators that best fit your business context;

3 perform a first baseline measurement on a significant sample of people or data;

4 decide on a method to improve this value (see the suggestions later in this chapter);

5 create a dedicated project for this purpose and name a person to be responsible for the project;

6 install appropriate software and measure or track your quarterly performance.

What are the indicators that drive the value of your TFC performance?

Here we suggest possibilities for choosing your TFC indicators. Choose the ones appropriate for your business, or come up with your own tailor-made definitions based on these examples.

Average time that a salesperson spends on selling to a qualified lead

A qualified lead is a potential customer who has expressed interest in a product or service and meets general buying criteria such as social and economic profile and past buying history. It is important to identify and target the qualified leads in order not to waste resources.

This implementation is quite straightforward, because it measures the actual interaction between the organization and the customer. The average time may be expressed as the number of hours spent with the customer, the number of phone calls that a salesperson sends to a qualified lead during one day, etc.

The sales force–customer interaction is calculated per product or per customer segment. The more the sales force is in direct contact with the customer, the more probable it is that the sale will take place.

Nowadays, the TFC is not too difficult to calculate, using modern contact management software. The required information can be collected from the daily reports or visit forms. If the technology is available in your organization, you can automatically gather the data by using software tools such as electronic agendas or contact databases. For example, many salespeople consider that targeting 10 calls a day to address their market is good value. If they achieve this target, it will help in reaching the organization's target revenues.

Sales activity accounts for sales results. This is why sales activity should be a key value to measure and improve your business.

> **Testimonial: The CEO of a small Belgian business in the consulting service sector**
>
> 'Every salesperson has to make 10 daily calls to prospective customers.'

Percentage of sales force people on your staff

The purpose is to measure the increase in the number of employees who have either direct or indirect interaction with your customers. The more your organization has people in the front office, the higher your customer focus is.

When performing a headcount on front-office staff, one must include not only all employees who are in direct or indirect contact with the exterior environment but also their entire support teams.

Salespeople per customer segment

A common rule of thumb in business states that 80 per cent of your sales are generated by only 20 per cent of your customers. This means that you must segment your customers into different categories in order to address them differently and be efficient.

You must therefore send your best sales representatives to tackle your most important customers and allocate more resources according to the customer segment that is most important in terms of revenues.

Opening hours and number of open sales points

The larger the interface, the more your organization gains customer visibility. Your opening hours, locations, number of points of sale in a certain region, and type of customer interaction need to be tailored to the needs of your customers in order to improve your TFC.

Adapt your business to what your customer wants and never participate in an approach that is not driven by customer needs. In order to get to know these needs, you could perform prior market studies, imitate your successful competitors or ask for direct feedback from your customers.

Average customer waiting time

This is the equivalent of inventory on a customer level, so it optimally needs to be minimized. The longer the customer waits (time in a queue, waiting time on the phone, the time taken to receive answers to e-mail requests, the time it takes to get an appointment, etc), the less efficient you are in delivering services, with a resultant lower TFC.

The calculation is simple. Just register these waiting values in your database and, if the information is not available, perform trials using fake customers at random moments and for different services.

Success rate of offers per communication channel

The TFC should focus on measuring and maximizing the success rate of your customer approach. The volume of bids that result in sales can depend on the communication channel that has been deployed.

The volume of offers can be the amount of products or services in pounds that a certain sales representative will address to one customer and for one certain product each month. The communication channel deployed to spread the offer can be a phone call, an e-mail, a personal offer in the mailbox or even a visit, and may differ for each product and each customer segment.

Using this figure, you can better calibrate your means of communication for different services and towards different customer segments in order to enhance your TFC.

Surface of display

This is a generic term to express the visibility of your organization to the market.

Notice that the TFC is not always measured in time. Depending on your business, this can be replaced by surface of the commercial space, the dimensions of your advertisement in the magazines you use for publicity, the indexing of your website on the internet, the number of potential buyers who pass by your window display, the number of prospective customers who read the magazine in which you publish advertisements, etc. The more you are open and visible to the market, the more you enlarge your customer pool and increase your TFC.

The communication budget

The percentage of your total budget allocated to communication can measure the success of your products and services. Communication is most certainly one of the most influential ways of attracting new customers. Think about it: a person who passes a big publicity poster, hears a radio advertisement or reads an article about your organization in the morning paper might be a prospective customer or can be the word-of-mouth link to another potential customer.

However, the communication campaign in which you invest must target the right customer. A meaningful TFC will combine an important and well-targeted communication budget with the sustained effort to better understand your customer, as discussed below.

The percentage of budget used to better understand your environment and customers

In order to improve your customer focus, you must first know who your customers are and what they want. Once you know your customers, things start to come under your control.

Some organizations blindly believe that they understand their customers well even if they have never allocated the budget to officially investigate this issue. There are many risks related to this belief, eg you may be missing a potential market segment, you may be losing customers to rival organizations or you may be wastefully allocating resources to projects that do not address the needs of your customers. Generally, the larger the budget for customer research, the more improved is your TFC.

Response time to customer requests

Your organization must be easy to understand and to navigate through for your customers. They should be able to find the appropriate information in the minimum amount of time, eg through a minimum number of clicks on the website.

If your organization answers your customers' requests as fast as possible, your TFC will follow.

The number of visitors to your FAQs

In order to increase contact time and especially its efficiency, a lot of organizations have website pages or other means of communication where the most frequently asked questions (FAQs) from customers are answered.

Customers interested in answering a certain question will have the tendency to check other questions that wouldn't have occurred to them otherwise. Customers will themselves improve the TFC of your organization.

The percentage of the organization's locations accessible to customers

You need to understand and know your customers, but customers also need to get to know you! The more customers can have access to your organization without encountering difficulties, the more they can contribute to your revenues, which is exactly what you want.

Examples of how organizations can implement this process include open-door days where they transform their offices into public areas, organization intranets or website forums, and a constant presence in the social media.

Customer feedback enquiries

You will improve your TFC performance by finding out what your customers think about you compared to your competitors. This information is vital for understanding your strong and weak points from the point of view of your customers. A simple feedback form made up of a maximum of six questions can be enough to achieve this information. In the six figure management (SFM) method we recommend focusing on the measurement of customer satisfaction indexes only in terms of satisfaction of your most critical customer segment and only for the most critical 'satisfying' and 'unsatisfying' features of your product or service. Using this 'spot' customer satisfaction index as your TFC indicator is a clever idea considering the cost–benefits of this measurement.

The number of customer-based indicators that you report internally

Many organizations have started focusing more and more on performance indicators that are customer-based. These can be internal indicators that certain teams within the organization use as a reference for their performance.

If individual incentives based on customer satisfaction exist, they are strong motivational levers. This means that employees will be more focused on customer issues if such incentives exist within the corporate culture.

Fast customer accessibility

A 24/7 hotline that is easy to reach, easy to find on the website or easy to remember should have the answers ready for the 50 most popular requests. This is a top-of-the-line TFC indicator.

Time spent answering complaints by the ombudsman

An ombudsman is a person who acts as a trusted intermediary between your organization and customers. Time spent resolving conflicts or dealing with unhappy customers is counted as TFC and may have an important role in customer turnover.

Enough time spent answering complaints can be the difference between a customer changing to a competitor and a customer who stays loyal to your organization.

The number of visitors to your website

This gives you an indicator of how successfully you've been reaching your customers via the internet. This is important, because it is a source of new customers, and more and more businesses nowadays are migrating towards virtual solutions.

If this value is high, you can publish it on your web page for everyone to see. You can compare this kind of TFC measure with your competitors' results if they have made them public.

You have a wide range of choices when it comes to finding the appropriate measure for your TFC. Once you've identified what best suits your organization, you can ask yourself the next question.

> **Testimonial: A commercial manager at a cosmetic goods company**
>
> 'Our web TFC is automatically measured on our website, by the number of visitors, the time spent on our web pages and the feedback, and enquiries to our dedicated section.'

How do you effectively use the TFC indicators?

Listen to managers experienced with the SFM method:

Use your TFC to urge employees to focus on all their customers, internal or external, present or future

Display, display, display. Out of sight is out of mind.

> **Testimonial: A commercial executive at a London-based financial company**
>
> 'The simple fact of the wide display of the six indicators that make up our TFC performance has improved our customer focus.'

Set precise quarterly objectives for your TFC...

> ### Testimonial: The CEO of an Italian mid-size company in the textile business
>
> 'The success of our business is due to the internal service–customer relationship in between all our numerous small service units. The TFC is a major performance indicator for us. It is measured internally and never falls below two hours per week on average for us!'

...and be specific and precise.

> ### Testimonial: The CEO of a large German commercial bank
>
> 'The TFC is essential for us. Our revenues depend on it and so does our survival as an organization. In the banking world, the TFC is explicitly measured, split by team, split by customer, split between customer and prospect, split by product. We have estimated that it takes 2 per cent of our sales force's time to gather and put together the information for TFC. This cost is negligible compared to the benefits.'

Focus your TFC on your most critical customer segment, internal or external

Focus your TFC on what's critical for you now, eg certain customer segments.

Testimonial: An executive at a Swiss private bank

'We measure and improve our TFC only for our most profitable customer segment, the high-net-worth individuals.'

Don't forget special 'customers' such as your suppliers...

Testimonial: A manager at a US trading company

'This year we decided that we needed to double our TFC concerning a certain category of 'customers': our suppliers. In our business, a good supplier and a good customer are equally important to us!'

...such as your employees...

Testimonial: A partner at a French mid-size consultancy firm

'Our TFC is calculated internally because our own employees are the most important customers that we have. They are extremely independent, autonomous, and we need to make sure that there is enough buy-in for our missions and objectives. We have doubled the amount of time spent listening to their needs and problems.'

...or such as your future customers.

Testimonial: A country manager at a US IT company

'We used to measure a good value for our TFC, but we recently noticed that we've been calculating it by considering customers with whom we are already in business. We've decided to augment the TFC by 20 per cent via new customer prospects.'

Reduce the cost of TFC measurements by sampling

We are not in finance, so approximations are good enough for clever managers to make wise decisions.

Testimonial: The commercial director at a large US telco

'The TFC is not difficult to measure if achieved by sampling. We calculate one value per team and always explain the great importance of this value for our organization.'

The TFC is one of the easiest indicators to measure among the six business figures. The results of your quarterly TFC must be made public in order to emphasize the importance of this customer metric within the corporate culture. Motivation of your staff will soon follow.

Before reaching any conclusions regarding the actions that you must perform as a result of TFC reports, ask yourself the following questions:

- Is the contact time between my organization and my customers higher or lower than in the past?

- Do we have the optimum amount of sales representatives to address the size of our market?

- Are my sales representatives proactive? Do they contact enough potential customers and are these potential customers the most likely to become actual customers?

- Is the interface between my organization and the customers (whether internal or external) large, visible, easy to understand and interactive?

- Are we well organized enough to ensure that our customers (internal or external) receive the answers to their questions and problems as fast as possible?

- Do we have the appropriate indicators to verify that our organization is customer-oriented to the extent that we target?

- Is our organization customer-oriented when we compare our indicators with those of other similar organizations?

- Do we measure at least one TFC indicator, and how accurate is it?

- Is our proportion of front-office and back-office personnel evolving in the sense of an increase of front-office?

- Are more than 20 per cent of our reporting indicators customer-oriented? Do we have a hotline active for more than 10 hours per day?

How can managers actually improve a bad TFC performance?

Imagine that you have defined and implemented the appropriate TFC indicators for your business. You have been shocked to find out that these indicators show that, contrary to what you might have thought, you are not customer-focused. Now you should do something about this situation. Here are some methods to improve your TFC.

Reward your most active salespeople

Individually track the TFC per salesperson and link their compensation to these quarterly results. Automate your process by deploying simple software. This will avoid tackling administrative issues each time you decide to gather information for your measurement.

The activity of a salesperson is the amount of time spent addressing the customer, weighted by the type of contact and the type of customer. Assess each type of activity through the type of contact: a two-hour face-to-face meeting with a qualified lead is worth more than an offer sent to an already existing customer.

Assess each type of activity through the type of customer: meeting an important, long-term customer will obviously be worth more than meeting a minor customer. Post the individual and team results so that everyone in the organization can see them.

Shift your business from back-stage to front-stage

This implies a progressive transfer of your personnel working in the back-stage towards the front-stage by either automating or subcontracting the back-office activities. By creating processes for routine tasks or by simply assigning these tasks to external teams, you free a lot of resources that can be brought into contact with the customer. More and more activities can be automated as you gain experience and as you grow as an organization. Take advantage of this process to bring more of your employees into closer contact with the customer. This will improve your TFC.

Increase the interactive interface between you and your customers

This can be achieved through window displays, shops, websites, call centres, sales force, marketing budget and sponsorships. Customers' interactive internet tools, extranets and extended enterprise applications will help.

Create a website that is complete in terms of information and easy to navigate through for the customer. Create forums, chat rooms and a FAQs page: anything that increases customer interaction. Internal or external social networks will help to boost the interactivity with your internal and external customers.

Testimonial: The IT manager at a mid-size company on the US West Coast

'The TFC initiative this year? A dedicated intranet web page for our project, more interactive than before.'

This applies no matter what the size and decentralization of your business.

>
> 'We have worked on improving our TFC by increasing the contact between our business unit and the rest of the organization through an intranet web page, publishing our success stories, voting for employee of the month, etc. We have managed to massively gain popularity within the organization, by doubling the number of employees who are aware of our activity.'

Equip your sales reps with some contact management tools

The following are good ideas that managers have had that you could adopt for your TFC programme.

Simplify your customers' visit report.

>
> 'We have had some difficulties with our TFC campaign this year, but I assume all responsibility for it. I had put in place a visit report form that was much too long. Our customers have all found excuses to avoid filling it in. Luckily, it didn't take us long to notice what was going on. We have optimized the form so that it takes less than a minute to fill it in, and it only addresses three topics that we consider essential. Today we manage to achieve an 80 per cent completion on customer feedback.'

Reduce the administration workload of your sales force.

'It's not easy to ask sales representatives to do paperwork, deal with administrative issues and fill in TFC reports on a regular basis. I have decided to take care of all these details for them in exchange for more support on the sales side. They get to do what they do best, and it has boosted business.'

Simplify your data collection.

'Instead of constantly following our sales representatives around, we randomly ask a proportion of them to fill in our forms. We gather the results from one-third of our sales force and consider a week's results for the entire quarter.'

Apply the open team agenda policy.

Testimonial: The managing director of a US start-up company in the entertainment business

'In order to calculate our TFC, our major performance improvement project for this year, we simply consult the agendas of our sales personnel. They all book their customer appointments in Outlook. As it is in our corporate culture to have an open network, everybody has access to each other's Outlook. It is consequently easy to render this calculation automatic. We therefore measure our TFC on a weekly basis by simply considering all the agendas. We compare our results and trace the evolution of this performance indicator by separating activities related to current customers and prospects. If the value worsens, then it's up to the sales force to bring it up again as a team. If one of the two activities is missing, the other must compensate for that lack of activity.'

Customer relationship management software will provide you with all the TFC indicators needed to boost sales.

Testimonial: The IT manager at a Spanish retail company

'We use dedicated software to handle our sales force contacts and we are happy about it. It automatically generates an activity dashboard where we follow the evolution of our TFC values on a quarterly basis.'

Include your favourite TFC visual.

> **Testimonial: An executive at a mid-size German transportation company**
>
> 'Here is the primary advantage of our customer relationship management software: the first thing that I notice is the weekly TFC value per product and its deviation from previous weeks.'

Create a well-organized and highly reachable call centre. This is an expense that usually turns out to be a good investment.

Hire an ombudsman. The TFC allocated to resolving complaints is always a good investment, which increases customer retention and creates positive word of mouth.

Create an extranet, the part of your intranet open to your suppliers and customers for self-help, to facilitate the knowledge flow between you and your customers. This is a low-cost method of growing your TFC.

> **Testimonial: A business unit manager at a national express delivery company in the UK**
>
> 'Our newly launched extranet has enhanced the quality of our TFC. Our customer visits have increased in number, and they talk to us far more than they used to before.'

Try to diversify your presence in the community. Be present on the radio, in the newspaper, on the internet, during important events, via your points of sale, etc. By multiplying communication channels between you and your potential customers, your TFC will improve.

Supplement your sales force in those areas where your TFC is low or where the customers are profitable

Increasing your TFC is expensive, which is why a good compromise is to focus on the essential segments of the market: customer, location, or type of product. Not all of your customers have the same needs and generate the same amount of revenue. By segmenting your customer portfolio more effectively, their satisfaction will increase and your profitability will be maximized.

A high TFC will allow you to know and differentiate your customers better.

Motivate all your employees to be customer-oriented even if that is not part of their direct responsibility

The TFC of your non-sales personnel can augment your total TFC up to 20 per cent. Incentivize and promote all non-sales personnel customer initiatives: complaint reports, suggestions, motivation to adapt to customer needs, etc.

What does the 'We are all salespersons!' slogan stand for? This is meant to encourage all employees, whether back-stage or front-stage, to sell their ideas and share their enthusiasm with the customers. For instance, a museum guide may very well make suggestions as to the general direction the public should follow according to daily interactions with customers. A delivery operative of an express delivery company can take advantage of close contact with customers to give feedback to the organization on what customers are happy and unhappy about.

Testimonial: A Swiss banker at a regional bank branch

'We have improved our TFC by simply boosting our sales force headcount, not by hiring additional people but by enforcing our entire front-office personnel to act as salespeople, whether they are working in delivery, maintenance or whatever.'

Reorganize and restructure your organization by market instead of by product

What's the definition of customer orientation in an organization? It is the structural shift of your organization from product focus to market focus. Prioritizing on marketing instead of production will naturally increase your TFC.

Increase the number of indicators in your reports that are customer-oriented

The index of customer satisfaction, repeat business indicators, and time to deliver are just some of the indicators that you can implement in order to be able to better measure your TFC. The high presence of customer indicators delivers a message to employees: we need to increase our TFC if we want to progress!

What are the limitations of measuring and improving TFC performance?

Be careful when implementing any of these measures, because they can sometimes be tricky and misleading. You have to make the best compromise between the advantages and disadvantages of your TFC.

The fake TFC

When measuring your TFC, you can easily be misled into including fake values in your accounting. Fake TFCs include: spamming customers with non-customized offers; a wasteful lunch with a customer who is a very easy catch or a non-qualified lead; a call centre that is always busy; and so on.

How do you avoid including this misleading information in your quarterly results? Be precise when describing what counts and what does not count as a TFC value. The definitions have to be very clear in order to avoid inaccurate results that are dangerous because they can attract misleading business decisions.

The opposition of some salespeople

Some of your salespeople will not appreciate being monitored through the TFC. Some of your back-office employees will show resistance to embracing the organization policy, especially if they are not experienced in sales or simply do not want to have customer interaction. If you manage to create an organization culture that encourages high customer focus, these opposing employees will gradually disappear.

The administrative overhead of implementing TFC

Measuring and calculating TFC can sometimes generate a heavy workload for employees. How do you avoid this problem? Do not measure everything: sample your measurement. Automate through customer relationship and contact management software solutions.

CASE STUDY 4.1 An integrated approach to the SFM method

Selling world-class consumer products takes more than a great sales team. A Swiss consumer products company knew that it also required the implementation of the right performance indicators. These indicators should be able to act as incentives for employees to increase their customer closeness and be able to satisfy customers' needs on the spot.

The company was searching for ways to improve its TFC performance, in order to enhance the interaction experience between customers and salespeople.

> *We implemented the SFM project starting with the TFC performance improvement, which improved our customers' experience while increasing our sales results... Our first TFC performance improvement was to cut our response time in handling customer inquiries. That is one of the primary ways we measure our TFC performance... We started out with our most critical sales channel, the call centres that customers use to place orders, obtain product information, and make returns and exchanges. Distributors also use them for the same purposes.*

Until recently, the company measured many indicators and used different metrics to measure its sales results and activities. It took too long for top executives to understand whether the company was really on its way to becoming more consumer-oriented. There was also no clear metric per customer segment, although the company was interested in approaching each of its six segments in a tailored fashion.

In a nutshell, the company needed to simplify its performance metrics by using the SFM method, with TFC applied per customer segment.

Middle management was also interested in promoting this initiative. This is because assessment was one of its main responsibilities and it was having trouble identifying the performance levels of the sales force. Former indicators based on sales were not very relevant because of the high dependency on external factors. The SFM method thus became a request at middle-manager level as well.

To gain the time and the money necessary for the sales force to be able to improve their different TFC performance areas, the second phase of the SFM implementation would focus on measuring and improving the sales department's gains from processes (GFP) performance.

> For a lot of good reasons, our SFM project consisted of integrating our many KPIs under a single umbrella. This really centred our focus on profitable growth. We used three indicators for this. The first one, TFC, was simply tracking the execution of our customer orientation strategy at the centre of the new scoreboard. The second one, GFP, was an indicator measuring our ability to free resources for that new customer orientation. The third one, key project status (KPS), was an indicator measuring the status of our key project in order to move our employees from the back of our company to the front.
>
> Our company first considered the many business performance measurement methods and scorecards, but we were impressed by the simplicity of the SFM method, which seemed basic but essential and exhaustive for any business. When we discovered it, we knew that it was time to get back to basics, to get back on our feet.
>
> We very much appreciate the benefits that the SFM method brought to our middle managers. They had been struggling for so long to find metrics that fitted both the top-down strategy and the request from first-line managers for actionable indicators. That was crucial.

The SFM method is so straightforward that for the implementation the company requested a two-day seminar only, conducted by an external consultant certified for the SFM method.

Nowadays, on a weekly basis at the company, middle managers employ the SFM scoreboard to keep the first-line managers on track and to translate the local strategy into activities. 'Thanks to the different measurements and improvements of our TFC performance, customers are happier. This is also due to the extended contacts they have with us and to the reduced waiting time.'

In addition, going with the SFM scoreboard makes it easier for middle managers to motivate and reward first-line managers. 'Since the SFM KPIs are more actionable than financial results, but still important profit drivers, a smoother control on first-line managers has led to more successful business units.'

Summary

The second step is now over; you are going to make the right innovations.

What's next

In the next chapter, we will review the third step of your growing strategy: getting the resources to move on.

05

Do the same thing but with reduced costs and delays

Measuring and improving your gains from processes performance

KEY LEARNING POINTS

- You will find out how to effectively improve the efficiency of your organization's processes.

- You will be able to choose the best gains from processes in your particular situation.

- You will learn how to improve your gains from processes once you've started measuring them.

We again meet Mark, the young manager from a typical company. His more experienced friend John is his mentor and guides him through times of trouble. In this particular story, Mark is the sales strategy manager of a retail company. In his quest to be innovative, Mark decides to invest in every opportunity that he encounters, without really taking the time to understand how he can use his prior experience to process things better, with reduced costs and delays and with the same quality. After a couple of months of intense activity, he noticed that this wasn't working out well for the company. Let's discover how Mark decided to apply gains from processes in order to solve these professional issues.

Things were not going well for Mark. Permanently venturing into new challenges, he was acting in a way that was causing his organization to lose money. He contacted John. John thought about it for a moment and then asked him the following three questions: 'Before embarking on a new project, do you ever think of writing down the ideal process through which to reproduce your previous projects, faster and more cheaply than before?' 'Do you invest enough energy in reducing costs and enhancing the quality of your activities?' 'Have you ever thought about reducing your efforts by 10 per cent each year through delegating or automating recurrent tasks?'

Mark was not efficient. He had been investing a lot of time and the organization's money in projects that were slow and expensive. He was not using his prior experience in automating tasks that had already been employed several times before. He was treating every new venture as if it were the first, without capitalizing on prior experiences.

Mark decided it was about time that he put some effort into redeeming himself. He started writing processes for his activities.

It was not an enjoyable task. However, the results were so successful that he thought it was worth applying and scaling this method to the organization level. The associated performance indicator would be called gains from processes (GFP).

CASE STUDY 5.1

In a particular German manufacturing company, the rules regarding new activities are clearly set out. All new activities are initially organized as projects. All projects that have reached their objectives are transformed into processes to reduce costs and delays but at equal quality. All processes are either automated or outsourced so as to be as efficient as possible.

CASE STUDY 5.2

A Swiss consumer goods company has recently realized that 85 per cent of its activities are repetitive and that the problems they are addressing are predictable and often recurrent. They are always facing the same delay issues, have the same demands and are asked exactly the same questions. In order to save time and guarantee constant-quality output, the company reinforced their processes, taking all recurrent activities and writing down the steps to follow, with a practical user guide for frequent issues. In order to track the efficiency of these initiatives, a new KPI was added to the cockpit, and it was called GFP.

CASE STUDY 5.3

An Italian fashion company has created processes for most of its activities in order to automate and outsource them. It decided to keep only added-value activities inside the company. It estimated that, after two years of rolling out activities within company premises, a process is sufficiently well mastered and specified in order to pass it on. The target is to reduce costs by 3 per cent using this simple transformation flow: 'project phase for first year, process phase for second year and out in third year'.

CASE STUDY 5.4

A US IT company considers that the main success factor for enterprise resource planning (ERP) systems like SAP is that they enable improvement in gains from processes. The ERP system provider for this company measures its client effectiveness through the same type of indicator.

CASE STUDY 5.5

A low-cost airline company spent a year figuring out what the best measure for gains from processes would be. It finally decided to go with the usage ratio of its three most critical resources, after unsuccessfully trying gains through outsourcing and gains through offshoring:

> We first identified the top three critical processes in our business unit. We wrote a document for each of these processes, describing the standard way of proceeding derived from best practices. The second step was to fix objectives for these processes. We have decided to go for cost and delay reduction of equal percentages.

Afterwards, we chose our GFP indicator. We selected the index of process complexity. Then we chose the method to improve our GFP. We chose outsourcing.

The next step was to automate the reporting query from our enterprise resource planning and a friendly graphical user interface for viewing the results. Our IT team was very efficient in delivering a fast solution.

The final step was to motivate everyone to actively contribute to our initiative. We did this by printing out posters with the results of this campaign.

The results speak for themselves: the delays were cut by 20 per cent and the costs by 2 per cent.

What are gains from processes?

Gains from processes include:

- reduction in costs through automation;
- reduction in delays through simplification;
- reduction in costs through subcontracting.

GFP measures your organization's ability to deliver quality at the lowest possible cost. You need to measure and improve your GFP in order to compete in today's highly efficient business environment.

What are *gains* in this context? They are any positive outcome that occurs as a result of standardizing your work flow, including increase of profit margins, cutting costs, reducing delays, increase of available resources, etc.

What is meant by *processes*? Processing means reorganizing and restructuring your work flow and value chain to achieve a specific goal.

Here is a quick checklist to guide you through the framework of processing:

- Initiate a process that precisely answers the needs of your organization's customers (external or internal).

- Write a clearly defined, detailed and referenced document as well as a checklist for verifying who does what. Make sure there is a clear decision tree of the sequence of things to tackle during the process.

- Decide on a target cost, time and deliverable of the respective process.

- Assign full responsibility for the process to a specific individual or team.

- Organize a progressive automation of the process.

- Sign a service level agreement (SLA) between all the stakeholders and make sure that everyone is aware of and agrees on the process.

By simply creating a process for a certain task, the efficiency of your work increases: obsolete steps are identified, inventory is reduced, costs and delays per product are minimized, the complexity of the overall work flow is simplified, and customer satisfaction increases.

Being a manager implies creating projects and ensuring results. Furthermore, you should transform your successful projects into processes in order to reduce costs and ensure stable quality. The next step is to delegate, automate, outsource and offshore your activities in order to dedicate yourself to the entirely new projects that require added value. The GFP value is the essence of efficient management.

There are two types of activities in your organization: new activities via projects and recurrent activities via processes. There is a rule of thumb applicable in any organization: 'Whenever the same problem occurs more than three times, create a standard procedure to solve it.'

To optimize their recurrent tasks, most organizations design different types of processes, depending on the activity you're involved in: production, sales, planning and management. For instance, the sales process plans all the steps, costs, delays and quality levels for a typical customer approach.

Probably 80 per cent of your organization's activities are either routine operations or standard solutions to recurrent, predictable problems. All these routine activities must be structured and optimized in order to enable the fastest results with a minimum cost and a target level of quality. Do not confuse this with quality enhancement, innovation and improvement of your product or service, which is only applicable for projects. For processes, the goal is to perform exactly the same task, but faster and more cheaply, while at the same time maintaining an established level of quality. These gains are measured through the GFP. The GFP value will reflect the image of your organization and the quality of your production and operations.

Open your mind. In order to be useful, the GFP should be adapted to your activities (see Figure 5.1). What are the equivalents of 'gains' and 'processes' in your situation?

FIGURE 5.1   Selecting the right GFP for your business situation

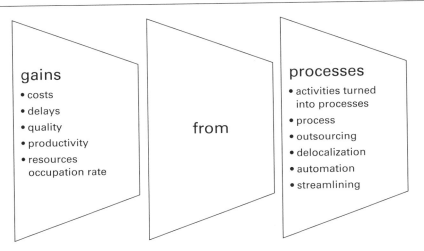

gains
- costs
- delays
- quality
- productivity
- resources occupation rate

from

processes
- activities turned into processes
- process outsourcing
- delocalization
- automation
- streamlining

'When we decided to implement the six figure management (SFM) focusing discipline, we first gathered our team together to decide what would be the three indicators that should monitor our GFP performance. We answered "Delay reductions" to the question "What sort of gains are the most critical for us now?" and "Outsourcing IT" to the question "What is the processing decision that fits our strategy now?"'

To whom does GFP performance apply?

GFP is especially useful for you and your organization when there are large amounts of tasks that are repetitive. This is likely to occur at a certain size of your organization's growth.

Here are some trigger situations that should push you into measuring and managing your gains from processes:

- when you have a large amount of routine activities;
- when you need to cut costs and reduce delays in your organization;
- when you are urgently required to move on from your previous activities in order to engage in new projects;
- when you decide to automate, offshore or outsource activities;
- when you need to boost your productivity;
- when you need to improve your overall efficiency;
- when you need to deliver on time, at standard quality and at stable costs.

Why should managers measure and improve their GFP performance?

Testimonial: A manager at a mid-size US consumer goods business

'We permit no tasks outside a clearly identified process or project.'

In today's highly overpopulated business environment, only the strongest players survive. Business books teach us that innovation is the key competitive advantage between business rivals, and yet innovation is not required in every business. Even when required, it is only possible if enough resources are available.

So the only common recommendation for any business is an increase in efficiency. By efficient business, we should infer fast, low-cost production for high-quality products and services. This can be enabled by effectively separating projects from processes and by further measuring the gain of your processes. GFP is therefore meant to measure and monitor the efficiency of your organization.

Why is it important to implement processes, meaning reducing costs, delays, errors and wasted resources in your organization?

- The organization is meant to create value for shareholders, and in order to do that you need to be efficient internally.
- You are always competing against somebody, and you therefore have to make sure that the on-time, consistently

good quality of your deliverables will make you your customers' preferred choice.

- The money and time spent on recurrent activities can be better used to foster innovation.

Managers need a measure for efficiency that is non-financial. Financial efficiency is merely a consequence of the organization's overall good practices. Managers need to directly measure the efficiency of their activities and operations by evaluating the GFP of their organization.

GFP is a simple management tool that conveys the following advantages:

- you now have a straightforward non-financial measure of your organization's efficiency;
- by simply implementing GFP as an organization strategic objective, the organization's value will increase;
- the set of processes that you have will help construct a knowledge database that will render your organization more resistant to a high level of employee turnover;
- people across your organization will be motivated to work more efficiently;
- the added value of each employee will significantly increase, and there will be more resources available for new engagements or innovative projects;
- all your routine activities will cost you less money and will speed up.

A high value of GFP for your organization might mean:

- there are a great deal of routine or repetitive activities;
- you practise outsourcing or offshoring;
- your organization is highly efficient;
- there are stable-quality, on-time deliveries and low costs.

A low value of GFP might mean:

- your organization does not have recurrent activities;
- your organization has recurrent activities but they are not efficiently managed as such.

Testimonial: The managing director of a business unit at a US consumer goods company

'Processing is the mandatory step before automation or outsourcing. It is indispensable to ensure that precise instructions are followed in order to achieve a desired outcome.'

How do you implement GFP?

The first thing you need to do is to identify to what extent your organization can make gains from processes. Separate your activities between routine ones that need structure and non-recurrent ones that need flexibility. The more routine activities you have, the more you can benefit from using processes. Organize your routine activities by using processes and your non-recurrent ones by using projects.

Here are a few practical steps for implementing GFP in your organization:

- Identify your recurrent activities.
- Write a specification document for each process.
- Decide what costs and delays you aim to reduce and to what extent. This will be a benchmark to which to refer when you analyse your monthly figures. Choose KPIs from those suggested later in this chapter.

- Define and create a dashboard to measure and follow your GFP evolution.

- Name a person to be responsible for each process.

- Start automating, outsourcing and offshoring the processes that are not competencies of your core business.

- Don't forget to include your customers and your suppliers in the process.

What are the indicators that drive the value of GFP?

Performance in business process management is not easy to monitor (see Jeston and Nelis, 2008).

Organizations generally choose one or more KPIs from those discussed below to monitor and manage their GFP. Use these examples to come up with customized indicators for your own business. Not all indicators are applicable to all kinds of organizations.

Percentage of process activities

As your organization grows, so will the number of process-related activities, functions, employees and budget. This percentage usually increases relative to the total activity of the organization, as the organization becomes larger. By monitoring and managing this growth, you control the efficiency of your resources, enabling a lean approach to running your business.

The gain from reducing delays in routine operations

You are probably aware of the three most critical delays that you wish to reduce in your organization. Delays are usually due to a lack of alignment of activities or to a lack of standardization in the way of working, especially when routine operations are the dominant activity in your organization. By better organizing your work flow via appropriate processes, you will manage to significantly improve your performance on delays.

Monitor your on-time delivery performance and use it to identify issues and manage your business.

The gain from reducing routine operational costs

From your experience in the organization, you know roughly where your most significant costs come from, whether from wasted resources, useless expenses or investments in activities that are unlikely to be profitable. If you have clearly defined processes to follow, these extra costs are identified.

The gain from outsourcing

When an organization reaches a certain level of maturity, recurrent and routine operations may represent a large part of the overall activities. These activities will be standardized into processes in order to improve efficiency.

The maintenance, surveillance and quality checks for these processes can be outsourced, because they no longer represent the core issue. The gain from outsourcing is generally significant, and it is a good measure of the GFP of your organization.

The gain from offshoring

You cannot successfully offshore an activity if there is no clear process specification to follow. You must define well and clearly state the actions to take and the decisions to make. Otherwise, the quality of your activity will degrade fast once you assign the task to a remote team. Offshoring is viewed by executives as a great way to save costs, and the gain can be reinvested in new activities.

The gain from inventory reduction

This is a typical gain that you can achieve from standardizing your work flow. By specifying the details of an activity, you can easily identify useless stocks. High inventory is a symptom of poor organizational skills.

The flexibility index

Extreme use of processes may reduce the flexibility of an organization. When reorganizing and structuring your activities into processes and procedures, you should make sure that your organization is still flexible by somehow measuring it.

Trial and error in routine operations

Even if a clear process is defined, this will not automatically ensure a positive outcome in your routine activities. The quality of processes in your organization can be measured by the number of loops it takes to get the work done properly, the cost of reworking, the cost of first employment of the process, the number of errors that occur as a result of following the process, the first pass yield, the reworking rate, etc.

The gain in productivity

Efficiency is a direct outcome of using processes. That is why you should measure the number of units produced per resource unit employed. An increase in productivity is a direct consequence of the increase of your GFP.

Investments in automation

Structuring your work flow into processes is the first step to automation. If you spend, for instance, 5 per cent of your budget on automation costs, this can be a measure of your GFP.

The overpayment index

There are people in your organization who are overqualified and thus often overpaid for a large part of their activity that consists of simple, routine tasks. Gains from processes will in this case occur from saving precious time for these employees, and reallocating the necessary resources where they are needed. The routine tasks may be handed over to an automated solution, an offshore team of less expensive workers, or a cheaper employee with corresponding qualifications.

The index of process complexity

The complexity of a process may be defined by the number of people involved, the number of steps, the location and so on. The more complex a process is, the more expensive it will be and the more the probability of failure increases. Reducing the complexity of processes is a priority for many executives nowadays.

The front-office/back-office ratio

The proportion of employees working in the front office is sometimes a direct indicator of your process gains. Organizations move employees from back to front when cutting back office jobs thanks to processing. This is, of course, only true for some businesses. A high-tech organization will have many employees in the back office, because R&D is not recurrent work.

The more your processes are working well, the fewer people you will need in the back office and the more you can concentrate on adding value to your products and services.

How do you effectively use GFP and what questions should you ask yourself?

GFP is a simple indicator to which everyone can relate. It enables managers to measure and monitor the efficiency of their organizations.

Once you launch GFP, be sure to clearly communicate the results to the organization on a quarterly basis. In order to fully understand the results, you need to pursue a detailed analysis of the GFP by digging deeper into the situation. As soon as you have the reports for the current quarter, ask yourself the following questions:

- are our gains from processing growing or diminishing?
- is this value higher or lower than for comparable organizations in our group or alliance?
- are we really using our resources efficiently?
- are we fully processing our recurrent activities or is there room for improvement?
- are the processes taking more time and money than they are actually saving?

- with the current processes that we have, are we still vulnerable to knowledge loss if key people leave the organization?
- what is the proportion of the organization's resources allocated to new unique activities, compared to the resources allocated to recurrent process-driven activities?
- where are the areas in which our organization can improve internally through processing?
- what should the organization be doing to make this happen?

How can managers improve a bad GFP performance?

The most popular methods for improving your gains from processes are as follows.

Overhauling your supply chain process

Our 10-year experience with SFM shows us that the cause of a low GFP performance, whatever the indicator you use locally to measure it, often lies in the supply chain organization.

Testimonial: The plant manager at a German automotive company

'Our GFP indicator? Reducing inventory. This is the best way for us to measure that our business is efficient.'

Reducing low-added-value tasks

Taking advantage of the SFM focus discipline, most managers rank their most resource-consuming tasks and activities on an evaluation scale from 1 (very low added value) to 5 (very high added value) according to the activities' contribution to the profitability of the business or to their estimated impact on customer satisfaction. Then the managers reallocate their resources and investments from tasks evaluated at 1 or 2 towards those evaluated at 4 or 5.

Testimonials: The chief engineer at a Russian manufacturing company

'We are constantly striving to achieve better results and to become more efficient in our business. That is why we never stop asking ourselves questions. How can we restructure in order to achieve faster and cheaper results? Can we live without certain tasks that only cost us time and money and do not add value?'

'This year's objective is to eliminate 5 per cent of our most inefficient activities in order to recycle the money and resources to invest in a new project.'

Ranking tasks, customers and suppliers by order of profitability

In accordance with the SFM methodology, managers measure the return per customer segment, the return per supplier type, the total costs of key asset ownership and the total costs per key activity. This method enables them to compare activities or contacts and to get rid of the less profitable.

> **Testimonial: A field executive at a Korean electronics company**
>
> 'Our GFP success story was finding the courage to get rid of a great many tasks, suppliers and customers that were slowing down our profitable growth.'

A two-hour team exercise

The benefits of measuring your different GFP performance areas are not limited to large units. Even a small team at a small internal unit will benefit from the discipline of reorganizing all its routines and all its predictable responses to demands in order to reduce delays and costs, while keeping stable and precise quality levels.

> **Testimonial: A team leader at a US West Coast plant**
>
> 'In our unit, we managed to carry out a very useful exercise. We wrote our team guide for local procedures. It took us half a day. We established a list of 20 recurrent problems from the most frequently occurring ones. We decided that the best way to solve each one of these problems was by rigorously following a checklist of things to do.'

Experts' debriefing

In most organizations, processes exist, but they are retained in the knowledge and know-how of the most experienced employees. A simple exercise, part of the SFM method, is to collect, write down and distribute this process know-how throughout the organization thanks to the GFP discipline.

Testimonial: An HR manager at
an Indian service consulting company

'Last year, when two of our best people left the organization, we were
relieved to have the description of the processes they had established,
in order not to lose the precious work that they had delivered for us.'

Outsourcing

In outsourcing, you delegate a business function or task –
commonly one previously performed in-house – to an external
provider. The idea is to cut costs and win time while preserving
the quality of your products or services. Your GFP will increase
through outsourcing, because you win time, money and resources to concentrate on core issues.

Many executives set as a yearly objective the outsourcing of
a certain percentage of routine, less profitable, non-core activities.

Service level agreements

If clear processes exist, you may expect clear outcomes. Make
sure you define a detailed service level agreement (SLA) with
your process provider. This SLA will act as a guarantee for the
quality of the results as well as an instrument to make sure that
the procedure is performed as described.

Offshoring

Offshoring describes the relocation by an organization of
a business process from one country to another – typically
an operational process, such as manufacturing, or a supporting

process, such as accounting. Organizations usually tend to keep their core business to themselves and offshore everything else.

If the workforce is less expensive somewhere else and there are lower transportation costs, but the quality of the products is preserved nevertheless, it is common sense to offshore part of your business.

Testimonial: A board member at a US steel company

'Offshoring has been the perfect solution for us in terms of GFP performance. A lot of our activities can be broken down into small tasks. We are producing work in four parts of the world much more cheaply, and we only carry out the final assembly at headquarters.'

Just-in-time delivery

In order for a process to be successful, it has to be well defined but also appropriately aligned with other processes. Make sure that, inside the organization, your processes are aligned. Rigour needs to be maintained for both external and internal processes in order for the mechanism to work effectively.

Enterprise resource planning solutions

Enterprise resource planning (ERP) integrates internal and external management information across an entire organization. ERP systems automate this activity with an integrated software application. Its purpose is to facilitate the flow of information between all business functions inside the boundaries of the organization and manage the connections to outside stakeholders.

By investing in an ERP system, your organization will automatically become more structured, favouring the idea of process.

Extranet involving suppliers and customers

Depending on your business, you may have suppliers and even customers involved in your processes. This is because these processes are often defined to satisfy a certain need of one or both of these parties. By creating an extranet, you will facilitate the integration of your customer and supplier contribution.

Bringing the front office to the fore

Every organization wants to be close to its customers. The tendency is to allocate heavy resources to the front office in order to get better alignment with the customers' needs. You can do this without adding headcount to your organization by simply automating some of the back-office tasks and using the newly gained resources to fill in the needs.

Improving your flexibility indexes

Measure and optimize your production line changeover delays, your workforce flexibility indicators, your engineers' multi-competency certifications and so on.

Testimonial: An executive in a large chemical company

'Our organization used to be very process-oriented and we were constantly suffering from the lack of reactivity to new demands. We have chosen to use the flexibility indexes as a measure of our improved GFP performance. We want all our processes to adapt to the very dynamic surrounding environment, in order to avoid over- and under-production and to be able to quickly change the product versions.'

What are the limitations of having a high GFP performance?

Misleadingly high presence of processes

Even though your intentions are good, blindly transforming every activity into a process is not going to bring overall gains to the organization. You have to carefully separate what is recurrent and routine from what is not. Otherwise, even if you seem to gain in the short term, you risk losing the minimum level of flexibility that is required in any business.

The closer you work to your customer, the more customization is needed and the less a process can do the work.

Becoming intensively rigorous and lacking flexibility

Flexibility is a key asset when it comes to aligning to your customers' needs. Even though being rigorous may ensure deadlines and budgets are met and a high and stable level of quality is maintained, there is a pressing need to be able to follow the dynamic trends of the customer. Finding a balance between flexibility and rigour is a key success factor.

Not thinking outside of the box

Take the example of the pilot who, facing a critical situation and having tried blindly to follow the procedures, finally escapes by finding an original solution to the situation.

You must always allow your employees to exit the procedure in the case of an emergency. Make sure that people are not trapped in your processes and that the human factor is still present in executing tasks.

Investing in non-profitable processes

Before implementing a process, you need to conduct a short assessment in order to make sure that the investment is profitable. Simply estimate the time and money that you need to implement the process, and compare it to the time and money that you expect to save. A rough estimation would be enough as the basis of a decision.

If you do not conduct at least a minimum investigation, you risk losing a great deal of money and time in formalizing processes that will not bring any gains.

Vulnerability to copycats

The higher your GFP is, the more likely it is that you have a lot of recurrent activities that are structured in processes. Having a knowledge database is very good if you want to preserve your skills without being dependent on key people.

However, a business model can be easily copied if everything is rigid and specified in detail. The real value of an organization is given by its inimitability.

Reduction of non-critical costs and delays

Over-optimizing your business may seem profitable in the short term, but it may lead to unwanted long-term effects. If your employees are harassed and bullied for every minor process misalignment, and you become too strict about everything, this may result in a bad working environment and even high employee turnover in the long run.

You should only define processes for critical activities that imply major cost and time savers in order to hedge this unwanted risk.

CASE STUDY 5.6 An integrated approach to the SFM method

To improve business intelligence and streamline operations, a small Italian manufacturer worked with us to implement the SFM method, with emphasis on measuring and improving its different GFP performance areas. 'Today, our business runs with less control and more motivated managers', says the CEO.

One of the team's responsibilities is to deliver scoreboards to more than 20 process managers throughout the company. The company's scoreboards – based on the balanced scorecard concept – were starting to falter. Managers overwhelmed the tool with too many KPIs, causing confusion.

Searching around for a new way to approach enterprise reporting, the CEO attended a seminar on human intelligence and the six figure management method. As he knew how to fly a plane, he quickly understood the quality of decision that a simple six figure panel could bring to the company.

The reason the company struggled with its scoreboards was because its employees had not come to see the value of that kind of business reporting, and financial indicators or production volumes did not motivate them. What they needed was a more action-oriented type of reporting.

We recommended the implementation of the SFM programme, and the CEO was very enthusiastic about it. He liked the fact that it was a simple and robust application. It gathered information from many sources in order to populate the different indicators. Similar to a pilot's dashboard, the panel enabled managers to visualize the entire performance of the company at a glance.

The CEO saw that SFM would help him to manage his process supervisors better, while keeping them free to adapt quickly in the field. He requested that, besides the main indicator, GFP, people responsibility level (PRL) and return on critical resource (RCR) should also show on the main scoreboard for his SFM reporting.

Implementation took days rather than weeks or months thanks to the simplicity of the SFM application. It was presented and assimilated in less than two days by the IT and control team of the company.

Almost immediately, managers were able to measure their gains from processing using their reporting tool. They were able to follow up on the new operational strategy of 'project–process–delegate' to gain time and money at a stable target quality. Reductions in costs and delays in processing activities soon became significant.

With our old scoreboards system, following our strategy involved a bit of guesswork and a lot of complexity. With SFM, we have greater control on the tipping points, from field activities to financial results. Field engineers see the benefits of the new metrics as well. One of the primary advantages – when compared to the old scoreboard – is that they can now see and act on the midway results that involve them in the success of the whole company, so they can do their jobs more effectively.

The different GFP measurements help increase operational efficiency: 'We use the different GFP indicators – like gains from processing in our supply chain or gains from subcontracting low-added-value activities – to focus employees on the most profitable tasks. The SFM applications recombine all the data centrally. We can then use the data for subsequent analyses to gain insight into our GFP performance.'

Summary

The third step is now over; you have the resources for innovation.

What's next

In the next chapter, we will review the fourth step of your growing strategy: investing those resources in the right people.

Give more to the best people

Measuring and improving your people responsibility level performance

Let's resume the story of Mark, the young manager from a typical company. His more experienced friend John is his coach and guides him through times of trouble. In this particular episode, Mark is responsible for a team of over 20 people, but certain characteristics of his leadership style are not best suited to making the most of these resources. Let's discover how Mark decided to apply the people responsibility level in order to solve his professional problems.

Mark is facing trouble within his team. Even though he is in charge of managing a good selection of bright young people, the overall results are disappointing. On top of that, motivation is low and employee turnover high. 'Nevertheless,' he thinks, 'the company is offering extremely attractive salaries for a very light schedule.'

Mark decided to talk to John. John thought about it for a moment and then asked him the following questions: 'How do you reward and motivate your employees?' 'How autonomous are your employees and what is the level of control and supervision that you impose within your team?' 'Did you know that, by granting higher responsibility and decision-making authority to your employees, you might increase their motivation more than by a rise in salary?'

Mark realized what was going on. He wrongly thought that, by close supervision and control, he would manage to achieve the results he wanted. He was using salary levels and bonuses as a source of motivation but did not realize that what some people actually wanted was more autonomy and higher responsibility. The outcome was low employee dynamics and high management costs. In the end, this had led to high employee turnover and very poor overall results.

As soon as he had identified the problem, the solution followed. Mark needed to change his management style radically.

However, as you may know from your own experience, this isn't a very easy thing to do right away, because it means a lot of changes in behaviour and a total turnaround of mindset. However, there were a couple of things that Mark could do in the short term. He would spend less time and money micromanaging everyone in his team and would grant more responsibility to those team members who both wanted and deserved it. He would find out (from quarterly interviews) what it was that each employee really wanted and try to tailor-fit incentives based on that. Motivation and dynamism rose within the team, although it took a while. Mark's reputation steadily shifted from highly authoritarian to that of an inspiring leader and guiding mentor. The business results were surprisingly good in the following year, and more and more people were sending in CVs in the hope of receiving a position within the team.

Mark's results were good enough to apply them to a higher scale, and so people responsibility level (PRL) soon became a strategic objective for the organization.

CASE STUDY 6.1

A hotel chain considered that their most valuable employees were the ones sitting at the front desk who had managed to sell at the highest possible rate the available rooms and suites. These top sellers had been given the responsibility to improve revenue for the most profitable rooms and suites. Their bonuses increased in order to reflect this upgrade in responsibility.

CASE STUDY 6.2

A branch of an international pharmaceutical company decided to use the management review committee method in order to assess the performance of its employees, because only by creating this type of multi-viewpoint procedure would the employees benefit from an honest and objective assessment. In addition to that, managers would each dedicate an hour from their busy schedules to listen to and advise those employees who got an AAA rating.

CASE STUDY 6.3

A US bank started focusing less on budget planning and more on creating full business cases. Only after managers roll out a successful business plan is their budget increased. The arguments for receiving an enhanced budget are now fact-based and less political.

CASE STUDY 6.4

Within a Washington, DC service company, all employees who reach their improvement targets, which they have set themselves, automatically receive more resources to achieve future objectives. This is a great incentive programme for taking ownership of and responsibility for targets, as opposed to coming up with objectives that are not realistic.

CASE STUDY 6.5

A German car manufacturer performs weekly employee evaluation and moves the 5 per cent who are the poorest achievers towards less critical and more closely managed positions. The 5 per cent who achiever most are promoted to higher-autonomy positions.

What is the people responsibility level?

The PRL includes:

- more autonomy for high-potential employees;
- more accountability for the best employees;
- more budget allocation for top performers.

Testimonial: A first-line manager at a Brazilian aircraft manufacturing company

'I always seek to increase the autonomy of my collaborators. I regularly ask them what type of decisions they would like to undertake in their teams, and I sometimes let them. I've noticed that an extra responsibility will encourage them to become even more cautious about the outcome of their actions. I rarely experience failures when I empower people. If I trust them, it is because they've earned my trust and they usually continue living up to that.'

PRL measures the organization's ability to provide the best people with more resources: more budget, more collaborators, more authority, more locations or more freedom. *People empowerment level* is another term for the same concept: give more to the best people (see Beine, 2006).

Even the best leader is very unlikely to predict, influence and control all behaviours within an organization. The human factor is the most difficult thing to manage, because people are fundamentally different and unpredictable. There are, however, several tips that you can use in order to increase human resource efficiency in an organization. Measuring and managing your PRL is one of these methods.

PRL is about ensuring that your high-potential employees get trust, responsibility and autonomy. By constantly detecting high-potential employees and progressively conferring more authority on them, you ensure a simple and effective way of managing your organization, as well as a prosperous future. That is why PRL has increasingly become a trend in HR departments nowadays.

What's your own equivalent for PRL? Who are your best people? What kind of new responsibilities or resources will you let them manage? (See Figure 6.1.)

FIGURE 6.1   Selecting the right PRL for your business situation

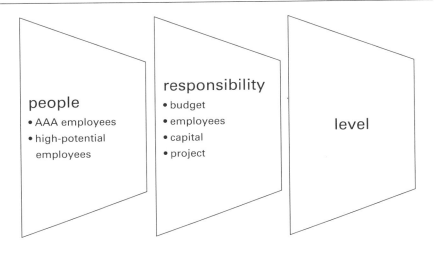

To whom do the PRL indicators apply?

1 *To your team.* How autonomous are your team members? Do you manage to distribute responsibility throughout the team effectively? Are people in your team motivated to act in the interest of the organization?

2 *To your organization, whether it is publicly or privately held.* What is the overall trust level inside your organization? Are responsibilities being shared within high and low levels of management and among employees?

Why should managers measure and improve their PRL performance?

There is no magic formula that will enable managers to achieve the desired outcomes from their teams. What managers can do, however, is promote a certain culture in order to stimulate better performance and greater initiative. More autonomy and more responsibility given to the right people are important success levers for an organization. All this can be measured and managed through the PRL indicator.

There are certain symptoms that show you, as a manager, that it is time to apply PRL in your organization. These symptoms should trigger the implementation of PRL, and include the following:

- your employees lack motivation, there is an increasing level of absenteeism and there is high turnover, especially among people you wish to keep;

- you have overqualified employees who lack exciting tasks because they are too busy micromanaging their teams;

- you have detected a pool of high-potential employees;

- your organization has a very sophisticated organizational chart with too many hierarchical levels, and you would like to simplify this process;

- there is a general lack of leadership and initiative, and employees are too used to executing orders instead of coming up with new ideas;

- you are trying to make your organization evolve, so you need more people from inside the organization to stand up and challenge the business model;

- your workload is very high and there is an urgent need to delegate responsibility to lower levels.

Once implemented, the PRL can help identify and solve problems in your organization. As for other KPIs, the simple measure and wide display of your different PRL indicators will attract improvement.

A higher value of the PRL will result in:

- *An increase in employee satisfaction.* Research demonstrates that for a significant number of employees autonomy and responsibility come before salary on the list of motivation levers.

- *A decrease in costs.* Management costs are lower, as a more autonomous and responsible team of people does not require much individual supervision. Other important cost savings may occur as a result of working at home or at the customer's office, as more employees are entrusted to do so.

- *An increase in variable remuneration.* More autonomy could lead to more result-driven remuneration. A high variable part of the salary favours the organization, because it ensures that profitable resources are preferred. A high variable part also favours the employee, because it is a source of personal satisfaction.

A low value of the PRL means that:

- *The organization favours micromanagement over trust.* The way of working is very costly and ineffective and keeps top management from concentrating on the big picture and strategic objectives.

- *Your business is running on high costs.* Having unmotivated people will lead to low productivity and high employee turnover. Each of these is costly for the organization. Close supervision requires time and money, and a use of resources that could generate profit elsewhere.

How do you implement PRL?

PRL should be co-implemented with your HR team, because it is a human resources KPI.

There are two required steps in putting PRL into practice:

1 Identify your high-potential employees. In order to assign more to the best people, the first thing to do is to identify your pool of high-potential employees. This can be achieved through:

- 360-degree feedback, an unbiased assessment given by subordinates, supervisors and peers;
- looking at personal objective accomplishments in the organization, such as management by objectives;
- direct appraisal by managers;
- high achievements within the organization.

2 Choose your PRL indicator.

What are the indicators that drive the value of your PRL performance?

Testimonial: A director of a French hotel company

'For me, autonomy is equivalent to responsibility. If my employees want to be granted the freedom to make decisions, they have to accept the consequences of their actions. Their salaries will depend very much on their results. The organization's financial interests are now shared between us.'

In order to grasp the value of your PRL better, you must analyse the following critical factors:

- *Number of high-potential employees and their overall experience level.* Are the staff mature enough for you to allow high levels of responsibility throughout the organization?

- *Hiring policies.* Is the organization targeting enough people who have the potential to become autonomous?

- *Organization culture.* Is the culture allowing people to act autonomously or are the employees expecting top-down decision making and micromanagement?

- *Leadership style.* Are managers encouraging their subordinates to show more initiative and to work autonomously?

- *HR strategy.* Is there an alignment between management needs and long-term HR strategy?

We now turn to values that organizations measure in order to assess the level of responsibility that is shared within the organization. These measurements can take place once in a while, regularly, over a segment of your organization or over the entire organization.

The assigned budget level per employee

Two years ago an employee at a particular airline company could single-handedly sign for an expenditure of $200 without asking for additional authorization within the organization. Today the same employee is entitled to sign for $1,000. This is a way to measure autonomy in an organization.

In the past, you might have needed 10 signatures in order to spend $10,000 of an organization's money. Today you need only two signatures for the same amount. This evolution depicts the gain in the autonomy level within the organization.

Certain organizations measure these trends once a year in order to assess whether the level of overall responsibility in the organization has grown or diminished.

Testimonial: The chief financial officer of a US express delivery company

'We have allocated an emergency budget of $500 to our employees who have direct contact with the customer in order to immediately resolve urgent issues that might occur. Our customer satisfaction index has considerably grown ever since.'

Strategic objective responsibilities

The number of employees with clear objectives that are linked to organization objectives is a measure of PRL. If, two years ago, 30 per cent of your employees had clear objectives of direct strategic importance to the organization (responsibilities related to sales, bringing on board more customers or capturing a new market), and today the percentage has grown to 45 per cent, then your PRL in the organization has improved.

Variable compensation

Increasing the 'pay-on-merit' part of the total compensation paid to all employees is fully part of PRL performance.

> Testimonial: A senior manager at a Canadian forestry company
>
> 'If two years ago 5 per cent of your average total salary was a function of objectives and today 15 per cent of your average salary counts for your variable part, this is a clear sign of improvement of your PRL.'

> Testimonial: An HR director at a Swiss insurance company
>
> 'When we started the organization a couple of years ago, 15 per cent of total salary was variable. Today, 22 per cent of total salary is variable. This is because we consider our employees to be our business associates, so we all share the organization's losses and benefits. Our latest employee satisfaction surveys reveal that motivation has increased significantly. I am sure that there is a link between the two.'

The diminution of costs due to micromanagement

If you have distributed responsibility throughout your organization, your management costs should diminish, especially those due to supervision of team members and their tasks.

The 'cost to supervise'

The cost to supervise (CTS) indicator is a good proxy for your PRL performance. It is a very useful metric to optimize the necessary number of hierarchical levels in any organization. If your organization is divided into too many layers of hierarchy, a high CTS indicator compared to your industrial sector standards will detect it. Too many bosses and not enough workers is a symptom of bad PRL: too many supervisors indicate that your employees do not have enough responsibility.

'We have divided our employees into two categories: those who supervise and those who actually do the work. Five years ago, the proportions were 15 per cent to 85 per cent. This corresponded to a cost of management and supervision of 25 per cent of total salaries. Today, 92 per cent of employees are classified in the 'do' category and only 8 per cent in the 'getting things done' category. Our supervision costs have decreased significantly. This is simply because our employees are now more autonomous and responsible than before.'

How do you use PRL effectively and what questions should you ask yourself?

The PRL, however you decide to implement it, should be a very tangible management value that can be grasped by every employee. It should be supervised both by managers and by the human resources department, updated on a periodical basis (monthly, quarterly, yearly, etc) and operate as an active trigger for strategic decisions in the organization. The aim is to have a high level of PRL, which means that the organization has a generally autonomous staff.

When analysing the value and the evolution of your PRL, ask yourself the following questions:

- what actions have we taken this quarter in order to increase the autonomy and responsibility of our high-potential employees?
- have we detected the employees who are performing tasks below their qualification capability and have we augmented their responsibilities as a consequence of this observation?

- do our teams deliver products or services that are tangible, complete, valuable and directly useful to our internal and external customers?

- have our job descriptions been updated to include the latest responsibilities and clear deliverables for each employee?

- are our wages evolving from predominantly fixed to variable?

How can managers improve a bad PRL?

Employees nowadays have a totally different mindset from that of a dozen years ago. They are more likely to act autonomously if they are entrusted to do so. A recent survey shows that diplomas, qualifications and experience are beginning to make less of a difference for different employee categories. It is the leadership and initiative of each of these employees that are the main differentiators nowadays. This means that, simply through the imposition of a certain organizational culture that favours autonomous behaviour, employees are valued more.

Decision making and professional independence are part of our professional culture nowadays to a greater extent than they were previously. We tend to be more reticent than before about taking orders and about rigid hierarchy. Hence autonomy and responsibility have become recurrent demands. Expect a very high acceptance rate for implementing PRL in your organization.

Redesign jobs

Design jobs in such a way that all roles have clear deliverables of high value to the organization.

Include measurability in job descriptions

For all job descriptions across your organization, make sure you include clear and exhaustive specifications of all the facts and figures that will be considered to judge the job incumbent.

Testimonial: An HR manager at a Hong Kong-based bank

'We have recently redefined our job descriptions, ensuring that each employee has a clearly defined customer, internal or external.'

Replace team budgets with team business plans

Ask managers to propose their own internal business plan for their team or unit, instead of only worrying about budgets.

Testimonial: A country manager at a French IT services company

'Our teams are progressively becoming more and more autonomous. The resulting cost savings have been reinvested in buying the latest technology equipment for our field application employees.'

Subsidiarity

This is about bottom-up delegation and giving power to the closest. Problems should be solved at the lowest possible hierarchical level. Only problems that remain unsolved should then be delegated to the next level up.

'Our management has introduced a new programme called TRUST. This
means that each manager delegates more to lower management.'

What are the limitations of the PRL method?

Risk factors in increasing autonomy

Too much autonomy and responsibility may lead to high failure
rates, especially if your employees are young and inexperienced.
Be careful to empower only those who have proven themselves
capable of it and who want it.

Not everyone appreciates autonomy

People are motivated by different things. In your organization
there will be people who do not like to be autonomous and do
not feel motivated by high-responsibility tasks. Be careful to
include employees' preferences in your decision-making process. This is mostly because initiative and responsibility involve
risk, which some people try to avoid.

Too much autonomy kills the corporate culture

The autonomous teams that you have built may become too
independent and may decide not to act according to the organization's strategy. Be careful not to destroy the link between
these teams and the organization. You need to preserve the
corporate culture and maintain a certain cross-team coherence
that is necessary in order to move in the same direction.

Frustration among other employees

You have to make sure that, when you decide to empower somebody in your team, you have objective reasons to do so. If you raise responsibility levels for some employees, the others may feel offended, left out or treated unfairly. Sometimes it is unavoidable to get reactions of this nature. The only thing that you can ensure is a certain level of objective fairness.

CASE STUDY 6.6 An integrated approach to the SFM method

Foster entrepreneurship by measuring it

The managers at an international IT consulting company were talking about the outcome of the implementation of the six figure management method:

- 'The measurement and the improvement of the PRL performance included in the SFM method enabled enhanced employee decision making and delivered benefits such as improved employee satisfaction.'

- 'The PRL performance measurements, driving us to rapidly confer more resources to the best employees, increased the effectiveness of our human capital management and resulted in significant savings in the time and effort needed to manage people.'

- 'For a rigorous focus on entrepreneurship, the only way to succeed is to measure it. Our company provides employees with a clearly defined entrepreneurial work culture, where individuals are empowered with authority and responsibility for their work.'

- 'Decentralized HR metrics failed to meet the company's high expectations for entrepreneurship. Isolated HR scoreboards led to multiple and diverse people responsibility indicators.'

- 'We needed standardized, centralized human resources KPIs to support our entrepreneurship strategy.'

By centralizing its entrepreneurship strategy results on the PRL performance of the SFM scoreboard, the company succeeded in streamlining and unifying its recommendations to favour entrepreneurship at all levels of the company.

Culture change at a glance

The PRL part of the SFM scoreboard created a single source of information for employees and managers willing to introduce entrepreneurship indicators. By standardizing and consolidating all related indicators on a single scoreboard, the company created a solid foundation for strategic, efficient entrepreneurship.

The results of human capital management made visible

The consulting business is an extremely competitive environment. If we do not give more to our best consultants fast, either expensive resources are left to waste or the resources leave us. High turnover is common in our line of business. However, this is extremely costly because of the investments that we make in finding and recruiting the right people. We want to avoid losing our top talent out of mere negligence, so we give them what they need and sometimes even more.

Measuring and improving PRL performance are crucial to professional service companies, because human capital is their most important resource and it needs to be well managed.

Economic value added

A key indicator for the PRL performance scoreboard is manager economic value added (MEVA). This is a measure of return on capital per manager, describing whether the investor's capital under the responsibility of a certain manager is generating a return or not.

With our SFM project we were able to move EVA [economic value added] down from the company level, through to the business units, and down to the managers' level. If one of our resources is being underutilized, we spot it on the PRL panel and we ask him or her to be released from the project, because our EVA is being eroded. This way of working has become common practice here and has sensitized people to the idea that a resource is a costly element, especially for service companies.

Summary

The fourth step is now over; your innovation resources are in the right hands.

What's next

In the next chapter, we will review the fifth step of your growing strategy: heading for economic and social results.

Invest more in your critical resource

Measuring and improving your return on critical resource performance

KEY LEARNING POINTS

- You will find out how to improve profitability and efficiency quickly and effectively in your organization.

- You will be able to choose the best return on critical resource to measure in your particular situation.

- You will learn how to improve your return on critical resource once you've started measuring it.

Let's consider another story about Mark, the young manager from a typical company. His more experienced friend John is his coach and guides him through times of trouble. In this particular story, Mark is the CEO of a software start-up. Even though his products are appreciated and of a high technical standard, Mark is having a tough time staying profitable. Let's discover how Mark decided to apply return on critical resource in order to solve his professional problems.

Mark had been losing efficiency lately. He was spending a lot of time capturing low-profitability business cases and not enough time on less exciting but profitable ones. His competitors seemed to be doing better than him although they were doing fewer projects. There was obviously a management problem here, but he could not identify what the issue was. He decided to talk to John. John thought about it for a moment and then asked him the following questions: 'What are your most critical resources in hand?' 'By what means could you evaluate their efficiency?' 'How could you increase this efficiency?'

Mark quickly understood what John was pointing out, and he decided to analyse his current situation. He figured out that his critical resources were his employees' hours of work, and that projects needed to be prioritized in order to fulfil the most profitable first and not to waste precious resources on those projects that would not bring much to the company. Efficiency could be increased, for example, by handling the difficult but profitable issues in the first part of the day and leaving the less profitable for the end of the day (if there was any time left). Another idea was to reinforce leadership and make sure that decision makers were aware of the return on investment of each project. Priorities should be clearly communicated across the company, and teams aligned to this single goal.

Mark then shared his ideas with the rest of his business unit, and a new KPI was put in place: return on critical resource (RCR).

CASE STUDY 7.1

In a law firm the critical resource is the few lawyers with unique expertise. The firm calculates its RCR as the revenues these employees generate every month.

CASE STUDY 7.2

A US pharmaceutical company, an ardent follower of the six figure management (SFM) methodology, decided that the most critical resource of the year would be the ownership of its medication licences, especially those with an expiration date of less than three years.

CASE STUDY 7.3

By strictly applying the SFM method, a consumer goods company decided that its critical resource was one of its brands. An analysis showed that a decrease in profitability was due to losing customer appreciation of this particular brand. The main focus was then to improve this brand's image over a couple of months. Everything else was second priority.

CASE STUDY 7.4

A French retailer decided that its most critical resource was currently the 10 per cent of store space that had the lowest return on investment. The company concluded that the measurement to conduct in this case was the frequency of clients per square metre over these critical areas in the store.

CASE STUDY 7.5

For a software start-up, the most critical resource was cash. It needed to make the best of every dollar spent. The gain in optimizing this resource was the number of days it could survive if it maintained the same cash burn rate. This RCR performance indicator was made visible in the office to remind employees of its importance.

CASE STUDY 7.6

For a car manufacturer, the critical resource was its supervisors, because they are hard to find and recruit on the market. The RCR measure that it decided to implement was the 'cost to supervise'. The improvements on this indicator were driven by the growth in autonomy of the supervised staff.

What is return on critical resource?

The RCR includes:

- profit per square metre;
- earnings per consultant;
- return on investment.

RCR measures your organization's ability to channel investments into your most profitable activities.

In order to survive as a business, the simple rule is to sell at more than you buy. Be careful to count all the overhead costs into what you buy, as otherwise you're out of business. Your overall activity must be profitable in order to satisfy the shareholders and in order to be able to reinvest in exciting new projects. Before managing your profitability, it is essential to be able to measure it.

Measuring financial profitability is essential for your business, but how could you go deeper into the analysis? How could you trace profitability from a more strategic perspective? The answer lies in measuring your RCR. By measuring your RCR, you capture more details in your profitability analysis. The RCR includes both profitability and its source.

What does the term 'critical resource' stand for? It very much depends on the activity of your organization. Criticality may refer to a resource that is rare, expensive, indispensable, highly profitable or strategic. Depending on the nature of your business, the critical resource may be your human resources, your capital, your locations, your intellectual property and so on. Your return on critical resource in these cases would then be the profit per employee, return on capital, profitability per square metre, profit per patent, etc.

Whatever you choose this indicator to be, the RCR will measure your efficiency in terms of resource allocation. The higher the value of your RCR, the more profitable you are and the more you secure your future profitability.

To focus on your most critical investments, the first question to ask yourself is 'What is my most critical resource or asset today and how am I making the most of it?' (See Figure 7.1.)

FIGURE 7.1 Selecting the right RCR for your business situation

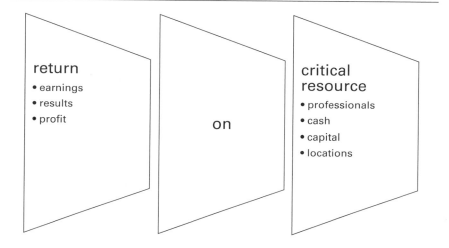

return
• earnings
• results
• profit

on

critical resource
• professionals
• cash
• capital
• locations

To whom does the RCR indicator apply?

1 *To you as a professional individual.* What are your own critical resources? What can you do in order to increase your own personal efficiency?

2 *To your team.* Are the team's resources used efficiently? How can you increase efficiency?

3 *To your organization, whether it is publicly or privately held.* What are your key strategic resources and are you using them efficiently?

Why should managers measure and improve their RCR performance?

RCR enables managers to capture and map the profitability of their organizations in terms of different key resources. Instead of merely conducting a financial overview of the enterprise, RCR enables you to create a more complex view of your organization, around different key aspects.

The measurement and management of the RCR are important internal tools that will allow you to control and prioritize resources. Resource management conflicts can be objectively settled by the use of this indicator. At the same time, by measuring the profitability of different drivers, you may derive tailored solutions that increase this efficiency. The more you invest in the efficient use of your capital, human resources, tools and collaborators, the more you secure your organization's future.

Improving your RCR is equivalent to wanting to be profitable and reinvest in your organization.

RCR conveys the following advantages:

- you will have control over the efficiency of your key resources;
- you will be capable of conducting a more thorough analysis of your organization's profitability;
- managers and even employees across your organization will be motivated to increase efficiency, because there is a direct link between financial profitability and internal activities.

A high value of your RCR might mean:

- a high level of overall profitability;
- good resource prioritization;
- good overall productivity.

A low value of your RCR might mean:

- the wrong internal strategy;
- unsuccessful execution of internal strategy;
- lack of efficiency of key resources.

How do you implement the RCR?

There are three easy steps in implementing the RCR:

1 choose which are the most critical, strategic resources for your business: activities, people, capital, intellectual property, customers, rights, suppliers, land, etc;

2 choose the most appropriate return indicator: turnover, gross or net profits, occupancy rate, social or environmental impact;

3 create a monthly, quarterly or yearly report and use the results to put into effect your strategic decisions.

What are the indicators that drive the value of RCR performance?

Depending on your activity, you may choose to implement your RCR in different ways. The following are some inspiring examples of what other managers use for their RCR.

Profitability per activity

Segment your business into separate, exclusive activities and consider that each of these activities is a critical resource for your organization. *Activities* may straightforwardly refer to business segments. Otherwise you may extrapolate the notion of *activity* to customer segment, supplier, technology or partnership. The main advantage is that this segmentation allows you to take strategic decisions that would otherwise be hidden in the overall picture.

Testimonial: The chief financial officer of a large Japanese manufacturing company

'We use up a lot of capital in our business, and our cost of capital employed is pretty high. The return on capital employed has to be at least twice as high as the interests that we pay for the respective capital. This is our profitability target per quarter.'

Brand value indicators

Brand might be the critical value to monitor on your scoreboard, especially if your reputation is in danger (eg unfavourable press releases).

Testimonial: The chief financial officer of a US consumer goods company

'Our most critical resource is our brand. Free cash flow alone can only provide a short-term vision of a business in general. That is why, on our performance dashboard, we have added two long-term indicators: customer satisfaction and brand value.'

Cost of goods sold

The cost of goods sold is one of the classical ways to measure your RCR performance. It is the cost of goods produced in the business that are sold to become revenue. By measuring and controlling these costs, you manage the efficiency of your production.

Social profitability

Your business might be focused on increasing social profit. This is not only because your organization cares about people and the environment but because of strategic aspects: this may convey a certain organizational image to your customers and employees, or it may attract government and union support.

If this is a major point in your business, you may consider measuring how your organization's different activities affect society and the environment. Social profitability may be specifically measured in terms of number of new jobs created, the environmental impact of your activities, toxic waste, radioactivity, preservation of green areas, social benefits that you create around the working area, etc.

Return on resources employed

If measured precisely, return on resources employed can help you understand your profit much better than from financial analysis. For instance, in the retail business, hotel business or any other business where space is important, the return per square metre is essential in understanding profitability.

> **Testimonial: An executive in a large UK consulting company**
>
> 'Our consultants are our key resource in the firm. As an indicator of our efficiency, we calculate the revenue and the costs per consultant, the revenue per working hour, and the profitability per consultant.'

Let's take the example of a totally different business: retail. The key resource is now completely different: the surface of your stores.

Gain per profit centre

If your organization is already segmented into profit centres, then you automatically have an available RCR. As a general word of advice, it is highly desirable to start implementing KPIs using the data that you already have. Once the KPIs have been put in place, their evolution should be pursued.

> **Testimonial: A planning officer at a Swedish retail furniture company**
>
> 'Our line of shops is our most expensive resource. Every quarter, we calculate the revenue per store surface and then benchmark it to different locations. This complements our financial summary, giving us a good indicator of profitability per location. We can then strategically decide what to do on a store-to-store basis.'

Return on your rights

All businesses have rights – intellectual property rights, patents, contractual rights, territorial rights – but few think about valuing them and measuring the return on them.

Testimonial: An executive in a large software company in Germany

'Our critical resources are our software licences. We make sure we calculate the return on these licences on a regular basis.'

Testimonial: The CEO of a US internet company

'The key resource for our business is made up of our captive customers, those customers who are loyal to us and reluctant to substitute our products with those of competitors. We are committed to achieve contracts that create a long-lasting bond between the organization and customers. Our methods involve high switching costs, comfortable long-term relationship maintenance or loyalty vouchers.'

Critical resource occupation rates

For instance, the square-metre occupation rate is a good indicator of RCR performance in the retail sector, but also in organizations where office renting costs are high. Another classical recommendation with the SFM approach is that return per senior consultant is critical to optimizing the global RCR performance of the consulting sector.

How can managers improve a bad RCR performance?

You have defined the most appropriate RCR indicators for your business. You have accurately measured them, and the results are clear. The next step is to take action and improve these values. Take a look at some practical suggestions for improving your RCR.

Replace your low-margin activities with high-margin activities

A classical method for improving your overall organization RCR is by abandoning your low-margin resources. You can start by laying off part of your staff, closing down certain locations, killing an activity sector and even discarding certain customer segments.

Another method consists of increasing the number of new products in order to address new customer segments. These new products will generate new margins. Novelty can be achieved by augmenting R&D spending or by acquiring and integrating smaller organizations together with their innovative products.

Segmentation of your most profitable resources

The well-known 80/20 rule of thumb states that 80 per cent of your profit comes from only 20 per cent of your resources. As soon as you have identified the resources (customers, products, suppliers, activities) that are most profitable for your organization, perform an accurate segmentation. Afterwards, concentrate on converting the other 80 per cent of your resources into this high-margin segment or on finding new resources to satisfy this demand.

Keep your core activities and outsource the rest

Your core activities are usually also the most profitable ones for your organization. If you sell services and you do B2C, then keep strategy, marketing and customer services and outsource all back-office activities. If you sell technology and you do B2B, then keep R&D and outsource your IT infrastructure. Don't forget to perform a profitability analysis of all your activities and alternative offers before jumping into this.

Increase the number of your profit centres

By scaling down the size and scaling up the number of your profit centres, you will achieve a more detailed picture of what is going on in the organization.

Valuation of sub-products

A sub-product is a secondary but useful result of a production process. You need to analyse the potential of these sub-products even though they do not have any value yet on the external market. These potential resources might be latent goldmines for your business.

Recycle your investments

As a rule of thumb, use 50 per cent of your gains from abandoning old projects to finance new ones. This will contribute to better integration of the notion of profitability per activity.

What are the limitations of the RCR method?

The wrong choice of resources

The essential step in implementing RCR is the identification of critical resources. If the selected resource is not really critical for the business then the results will be misleading for the business decision process.

Let's take a simple example from the fast food industry. Imagine that the employees are wrongly considered to be the critical resource in a national fast food chain. Lower results in turnover per employee will probably lead to increasing the amount of training given to your staff. You will end up spending money uselessly, without results. The actual critical resource is probably something else, location for instance. Choosing the wrong location for your restaurant may lead to a decrease in revenues. The employees have no say in this, as they cannot control external factors.

With the wrong critical resource in mind you might fail, for instance, to notice that one of your locations is simply non-profitable.

The overcrowded KPI picture

Some organizations may have multiple resources that they consider critical. By creating too many indicators, the performance dashboard may become very crowded and highly unreadable. This effect should be avoided. Bear in mind that the aim is to have a clear picture of your organization that will enable you to take strategic decisions.

The advice is to choose only the most important resources for your organization. Clearly define what you measure, how you measure it and when you measure and report it via an appropriate KPI card that collects the relevant information. If the dashboard is clearly defined, then the solution will naturally follow.

The non-exhaustive, non-exclusive resources

The defined critical resources usually only refer to part of the organization. Hence, when you analyse your RCR, you will have a non-exhaustive view of your current performance. The danger is that you may overlook important aspects of your business by concentrating only on what you've defined as critical. On the other hand, if you've defined two or more resources that are partially overlapping in terms of profit, then it might be difficult to relate the overall profitability picture to either of the two. Make sure that you never forget to relate your RCR to global financial profitability.

Moving targets

In today's highly dynamic business world, organizations that manage to move along with the trend survive, while those that cannot keep up eventually die. It might occur that one's critical resource changes over time. If the performance board does not also shift, then the strategic decisions that occur may be totally biased. Try to make sure that your RCR is always up to date, even though this might cost you extra maintenance work.

CASE STUDY 7.7 An integrated approach to the SFM method

The objectives of the SFM method at a French retail and distribution company were listed as follows:

- provide a single comprehensive view of pre-financial performance indicators;

- improve the operational reporting top view;

- enable motivation of middle and first-line managers;

- build in flexibility to select the relevant indicators that appraise global performance;

- simplify the different KPI scoreboards;

- integrate the performance from several departments into a single accurate scoreboard that predicts future financial results;

- establish standard key performance indicators for members throughout the company;

- improve visibility of the different RCR performance indicators to compare units.

'We had to create a KPI consolidation solution from the ground up', said the chief operating officer. 'SFM helped lead the way. To manage our point of sales and understand overall profitability drivers, we had to first create a dashboard for our RCR performance and then link it to our gains from processes (GFP) and sales from new sources (SFN), which are the indicators that are most correlated to RCR.'

Recognizing the need for KPI consolidation

Middle managers at the company needed a simple KPI cockpit linking the corporate goals with managers' activities. They selected the RCR performance project from the SFM method to lead the way to other KPIs.

Then they helped region and store managers to select the right kind of resource and the right kind of return to measure and improve. The previous scoreboard contained more than 120 separate KPIs, so even reporting for internal purposes was complicated and time-consuming. 'Our existing performance measurement processes definitely had problems: they lacked the leadership of the six figure management process. Managers would spend weeks discussing the right return to focus on. They tended to globalize the return on all resources, hiding emerging problems. Managers in different departments were not coordinated around a single, common profitability goal.'

Many managers were using separate metrics in the profitability reports, and there was no way to achieve a consistent company-wide set of KPIs that would reflect a clear common status. Without reliable targets for profitability analysis, managers lacked focus. Concentrating on the RCR during one quarter brought them back on track. Even if the critical resource changed over time according to their own environment, shifting from square metre, to cash, to top vendors, to key local supplier, to captive customers and so on, their contribution to group profitability stayed secure for the long term.

The CEO had seen the benefits of using the SFM method when visiting his suppliers, large consumer product companies that had been using this method for a while. The implementation started with a kick-off seminar given to the internal implementation team and presented by SFM certified consultants. The existing SAP reporting system was then tailored to the specifications of the SFM method.

Setting up an integrated top reporting structure

Selecting the indicators that will measure our RCR performance was a critical first step. We began by deciding what our main critical resource was today, in our situation. As expected, it turned out to be something completely different country by country, depending on our local strategy to fight competitors. The second step was to decide what was the relevant return to measure to really motivate the field managers: financial returns, occupation rates, volumes, etc.

The implementation team then aligned all potential resources and returns that it could be relevant to measure and decided to let the field managers decide, as long as their RCR performance stayed within the safe limits for the general profit indicators.

Profitability is now reported by square metre, by customer segment, by cash burnt and by key supplier. But field profitability drivers that are highly correlated to these indicators are also reported in order to be proactive: occupation rates, cost of goods sold, rental cost, etc. Different kinds of returns, financial and non-financial, are now visible for profit and loss accounts for critical resources: square metre, franchise, fidelity of customers, suppliers, managers.

The advantage of a thorough enterprise key field performance management solution using the SFM method is that the financial staff can predict financial profitability better.

Visibility of the RCR performance indicators provides middle managers with a pragmatic tool to compare their performance against prior periods, against established goals and against the competition.

SFM provides a level of simplicity for mid-management to further reduce the number of KPIs for standard reports.

Summary

The fifth step is now over; your innovation will make sense.

What's next

In the next chapter, we will review the last step of your growing strategy: making it happen.

Focus on one key change project

Measuring and improving your key project status performance

Let's consider a last story about Mark, our young manager from a typical company. His more experienced friend John is his coach and guides him through times of trouble. In this particular story, Mark had been a management consultant in his company for a year and a half, but people still didn't know him despite his good results. Let's discover how Mark decided to apply key project status in order to solve his professional problems.

Mark had not received a lot of attention since his arrival at the company. He was perfectly aligned with his job description and had achieved good results. Despite this, nobody in the organization seemed to notice either him or his work. When the organization had new projects, nobody thought about sharing any responsibilities with him.

He decided to talk to John. John thought about it for a moment. 'Your role in the organization should be defined by what sets you apart from others', he said. He then challenged Mark with some questions: 'What differentiates you in the organization, so that people are able to identify and distinguish you from your peers?' 'What innovative projects have you initiated within your organization?' 'What is the added value of these projects?' 'How do you effectively follow your project advancement?'

Mark felt that John's questions clearly pointed out his weaknesses. Throughout his career, he had not managed to associate his name with any remarkable projects within the organization. That is why, despite his good results as an employee, he had never really earned the attention of his colleagues. It was about time he initiated a project that would establish himself as a well-known name within the organization.

Mark soon took up a very challenging and risky project on his personal initiative. Carving out a clear plan, he managed to carry out his project successfully. Following this achievement, he launched a team project of strategic importance to his organization. He picked a time of the year when business was fairly low. That way, he could allocate more than half of his time to the new project, while the rest was sufficient to complete his regular organizational tasks. The reactions that he got were very flattering. After a couple of months of pushing the initiative, Mark was known by everybody in the organization, and people whom he did not even know were congratulating him on his success.

Following the positive results of this initiative, Mark thought it would be a good idea to apply and scale this method to his team and, moreover, his organization. Therefore he came up with a proposition to implement key project status (KPS) as an organization objective.

CASE STUDY 8.1

An executive at an express delivery enterprise decided that his main project for a quarter would be an aircraft overhaul project. He then decided that the most valuable indicators for following up this project would be the next specification deliverables. He focused only on this objective and delegated the rest to his collaborators.

CASE STUDY 8.2

An executive in a public administration company decided to concentrate her efforts on a single project in the coming year. Anything else on the agenda would be treated as a second priority and delegated to other teams across the company. She hung a poster on her office wall saying 'Is our new software project in a healthy state?' Beneath this statement, she put the six indicators that would monitor the state of her project, covering everything from cost to timeliness and quality. She also used this performance cockpit in her presentations in order to establish her leadership.

CASE STUDY 8.3

A company had recently acquired its main competitor. This project was the most important one of the year, because it directly drove the company strategy to become market leader. If this project was successful, market leadership would be guaranteed in the coming years. Dedicated project management software carefully followed the status of the project. The Gantt diagrams were made public on the company intranet for everyone to see and follow.

What is key project status performance?

KPS includes:

- on-time delivery for your most important project;
- deviances from budget for your most critical project.

KPS measures executives' ability to implement a key change project successfully. You need to measure and improve your ability to drive change inside your organization if you want to be aligned with changes in the business environment.

What is a *key project*? It is a high-priority project that is meant to align activities with your organization's strategy. It's up to you to decide which projects are considered critical. It is usually a good idea to concentrate on one key project at a time.

What does *status* refer to? It is about keeping track of the activities that you choose to set as high-priority. In order to implement change successfully, you must have at least a minimum of monitoring of the major milestones. Without this, projects are likely to end up abandoned or off track at early maturity. Nowadays, there are plenty of software solutions that help managers keep track of their project progress.

The higher the value of your KPS, the more you have the capacity to keep your organization in step with external changes, and the more you have the ability to adapt to your constantly fluctuating business environment. Increasing KPS will increase your fit to external constraints and needs, as well as improve your internal performance. By enhancing your KPS, you will consequently increase your market share and efficiency.

Testimonial: The chief operating officer of a utility company in Denmark

'I personally encourage my employees to come up with challenging projects. We have a programme called Innovation Cell, and every year the initiators of the best projects, which have shown good progress, are rewarded.'

What is currently your main key project? What indicator is the best one with which you can monitor this project? (See Figure 8.1.)

FIGURE 8.1 Selecting the right KPS for your business situation

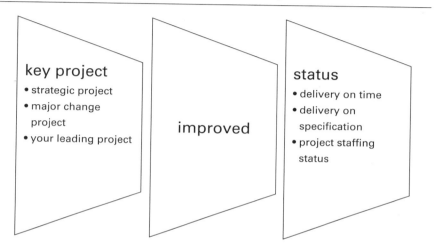

key project
- strategic project
- major change project
- your leading project

improved

status
- delivery on time
- delivery on specification
- project staffing status

To whom do the KPS indicators apply?

1 *To you as a professional individual.* You most probably have a professional roadmap in mind. What do you need to achieve in order to reach your objectives? What are your priorities in terms of achievements? How do you adapt your roadmap to environmental changes in the business world? What projects have you initiated in order to coordinate your actions according to these changes? Do these projects include a concept, budget and associated dashboard to track their evolution?

2 *To your team.* A team needs to evolve and permanently adapt to the requirements of the organization. New problems require new solutions, meaning projects

have different priorities. You should always be able to identify one or two critical projects for an organization. For these critical projects, make sure that you provide detailed planning that will help you achieve your goals.

3 *To your organization, whether it is publicly or privately held.* Is your organization flexible enough to adapt accurately to changes? What are the critical projects that your organization is undertaking this year?

Testimonial: A marketer at
a small waste management company

'I'm a pure marketing person, but ever since I initiated intranet knowledge management for our organization I've become very popular and all my colleagues throughout the organization know my name.'

Why should managers measure and improve their KPS performance?

Testimonial: The CEO at a US
automotive manufacturing company

'How do I lead this company? I focus on one key change and I delegate the rest. I've chosen a single large project as a priority for this year, a new market for us to enter. I've displayed a large poster in our meeting room depicting our weekly progress. The delays are highlighted in red for everyone to notice.'

Any business has a project or several projects. Managers need to be aware of the relative importance of each project in order to concentrate their effort on the key activities of their organization. Projects need to be properly defined and continuously tracked in order to achieve the desired outcome.

The primary role of a manager is to foster change, and drive change from strategy to execution. It is up to you, as a leader in your organization, to align your team to the global strategy. You do this by initiating and tracking projects within your organization. You need an indicator to tell you how you are performing on your key projects, because you cannot manage what you don't measure. This indicator is the KPS. If the indicator is green, it means that the project is on track and that the business unit is going to change, adapt and progress.

We tend to associate the name of the manager in charge with projects that have had great impact in the organization. That is why it is important for your professional development as a manager to undertake challenging projects of this type.

KPS might sound abstract at first, but it is actually a very tangible measure of your organization's internal and external success. KPS conveys the following advantages:

- Performance in your organization is now evaluated through the success rate of new projects.
- Your organization is openly tracking its main projects, so everybody is aware of the priorities. The employees will consequently adjust their focus on these key aspects.
- The individuals leading these high-impact projects will be recognized for their initiatives, contributing to the enrichment of the corporate culture.
- You are now able to link your organization's global results to internal failures or successes.

Testimonial: A team leader at a French catering company

'I work within a geographically dispersed team, and until recently we had a tough time dealing with numerous projects at once. As soon as the KPS was implemented, we became clearly aware of our priorities and of where we stand in our project progress. We are now motivated to work together towards a clear common goal.'

A high value of the KPS might mean that:

- a great many changes have been achieved according to the organizational strategy;
- key projects in the organization are on track;
- there is high flexibility and drive inside the organization.

A low value of the KPS might mean that:

- the need to adapt to a global strategy is blocked by the incapacity to deliver changes on an operational level;
- the amount of work in project management is keeping managers from performing strategic tasks within the organization;
- there is low flexibility to change within the organization;
- the organizational culture is very conservative and people are reluctant to change.

How do you implement KPS measurements?

The implementation of KPS is easy if you follow these simple steps:

1 Clearly identify the strategic objectives of your organization.

2 Agree upon or negotiate the objectives that have been assigned to your business unit as part of this global strategy.

3 Select a set of operational indicators from those discussed below. These are the aspects that you need to improve in order to achieve your objectives. They will represent your KPS indicator.

4 Create a project or an action plan to enhance the selected indicators, in order to be on track with the strategic direction of the organization.

5 Create a dashboard application to track the budget and schedule of your project.

Bear in mind that, in order to interpret the results, clear benchmark values for the KPS must be established by the organization, for instance by comparing with similar organizations or the main competitors.

What are the indicators that drive the value of your KPS performance?

It's not easy to quantify the impact of leadership programmes and projects (see Phillips, Phillips and Ray, 2012). We propose the KPS as a potential KPI for evaluating this management orientation.

Some of the most popular examples from which to choose the appropriate indicators to measure your KPS are discussed below.

Quarterly deviations

Each quarterly deliverable will be described by a series of measurable results. Calculating the deviation from the target should not be an issue.

Project schedule deviation

When a project is defined, the resources for the project need to be available at a specific date. The milestones need to be delivered on specific dates. Measuring the deviation from the baseline, once all these values are available, is a very straightforward and easy operation.

Project·budget deviation

Whenever a project is defined, the budget for every milestone is also clearly stated. It is therefore easy to measure the deviation of what you actually spend with regard to the target values.

Earned value management

Earned value management is a very popular project management technique for measuring project performance and progress in an objective manner. It has the ability to combine measurements of scope, schedule and budget in a single integrated system. Therefore, if you want to really grasp the deviation of your project by combining both schedule and budget, this is a very clean and accurate way to do so.

The availability of key actors

Any complex project within an organization requires the collaborative work of many people. Sometimes a couple of hours of workload can be the bottleneck of a project if the required stakeholders are not available. The resource gaps may be tracked and reported easily if a list of stakeholders and tasks is created at the beginning and tracked on a quarterly basis.

The project indicators

A project is meant to solve an issue or a series of issues within the organization. Consequently, the outcome of a key project will usually be reflected in the value of one or several performance indicators. If these indicators do not progressively improve as a result of the project effort, then the KPS can be asserted as red.

Once you have followed these simple steps, calculate your KPS on a quarterly basis and post the results for all employees to see. This is both informative and motivating for your entire corporation.

Testimonial: An engineer at a water distribution company

'My personal project consists of introducing a process that will reduce costs to up to a couple of percentage points while preserving quality.'

What questions should you ask yourself?

The KPS can be both a measurement of your performance and a motivational tool. Your KPS can influence your staff to prioritize on certain projects rather than on others.

If you are a manager trying to analyse your KPS quarterly results, start by asking yourself the following questions:

- what is my organization strategy this year and how does my business unit contribute to this?
- what are the key projects that will enable the success of this strategy on a business unit level?

- what dashboard should I track and how can I implement it effectively?
- what are the resources I need in order to deliver this project successfully?
- what are the other KPIs that each project will influence and what are the expectations for this?
- if the performance indicators do improve as expected, does this mean that the strategic objectives have been achieved?
- how do I communicate the importance of a project in order to motivate the employees to focus on it?

How can managers improve a bad KPS performance?

You have defined a KPS for your business. You have accurately measured it on a quarterly basis. Now you've noticed that your performance could do with improvement. What are the most popular methods that you, as a manager, can apply to improve your KPS?

Testimonial: The country manager of a large US internet company

'I have an excellent number two to whom I can confide all operational work. I am 100 per cent dedicated to strategic issues and change management.'

Concentrate entirely on your key project and delegate the rest

A large key change project often requires a tremendous amount of energy, especially from its coordinator. Choosing to lead a single large key project at a time is a good idea if you want to maximize its success rate. On an organization level, this can mean outsourcing non-core activities and keeping only those projects of critical importance. Some organizations call this the 'make or buy' strategy.

Testimonial: The managing director of a mid-size business unit at a large food product company

'Our secret is our focus. Ever since we've been concentrating on our top-selling product, we have become the number one nationwide and we've gained unexpected amounts of market share.'

Rigorously fill in the master project document before launching the project

The master project document includes a checklist of classical questions that need to be answered before authorizing the launch of any project. Examples include:

- with what tangible results will we see that this project is a success?
- what problem will be solved if this project is a success?
- what are the project's objectives?
- who are the customers of the project?
- what are the expenses and what are the deadlines?
- what are the specifications of the quarterly deliverables?

- what are the risks involved?
- what are the exit points of the project?

Use adapted project management software

Nowadays, there are plenty of project management tools that you can use, which can adapt to the project size and type. They automatically generate dashboards or visuals that are indispensable in understanding the current status of your project.

Secure all the necessary resources that you may need for your project

Too many projects are launched without ensuring that all the necessary resources are officially available. This is a common mistake that is often fatal for the outcome of the project. It is very important for managers to be proactive in order to avoid costly project failures.

Testimonial: The chief operating officer of a major US non-profit organization

'I never approve a project unless it has a clear scope, detailed research on risks and opportunities, and precise planning. The cost of failed projects is too high to accept the risk.'

Name a full-time project manager

Any project of critical importance should have a dedicated project manager. You, as a manager, should concentrate on management and leave the technical issues to specialists.

Testimonial: A top manager of a Swiss
public administration body

'In my organization every large project has a dedicated project manager.
The project leaders are then free to concentrate on specific issues instead
of worrying about the progress of the project itself.'

Increase the visibility of your project

As a manager, you must ensure that your employees are aligned
with the organization's priorities and are aware of the project's
progress. You must all have a common understanding of the
organization's goals and activities in order to act as a single
entity. Setting weekly or quarterly priorities and reporting them
to everyone are a good way to achieve this objective. Displaying
your project progress on a blackboard will keep everyone
alert and aware of risks.

What are the limitations of KPS performance?

Neglecting side projects

If you invest all your energy in a single large project, all your other
recurrent, routine or less important projects will be neglected.
Your business rarely depends on a single project, so be careful
not to destroy organization value by concentrating on a single
objective.

Misjudgement of priorities

Business is not predictable. Unexpected events may occur, and when they do it's good to be prepared and have some back-up projects to get on with. Sometimes side projects that seemed less important may become the nuts and bolts of the organization.

It's good to revise your priorities constantly and to keep some free space for potential projects. A misjudgement of priorities can turn out to be fatal for an organization, so take special care of this aspect and revise your strategy as often as possible.

Inaccurate measurements

As with any performance indicator, the KPS metric is useful if it is accurate and shows the facts about the situation it describes. Take special precautions, because a misleading KPS can have negative effects on your organization's performance. Make sure that the definition of the metric is clear and that the chosen benchmarks are in line with what you measure.

High-risk engagement

If you initiate an exciting project with high-gain prospects, it is very likely that your project is also risky. This means that, in the unfortunate event of failure, your organization, as well as your reputation, will certainly suffer. If the project turns out to be disastrous, you may even risk bankruptcy or getting fired. The price of escaping anonymity is high and can sometimes cost you your career.

Higher costs

Having a dedicated project manager for each key project can be very costly. Even though it is sometimes worth investing resources, you have to make sure that it is absolutely necessary. Only hire as many project managers as you need to cover major projects. Small projects can go without.

CASE STUDY 8.4 An integrated approach to the SFM method

Manager-led SFM implementation

This Swiss fine chemicals company decided to implement the six figure management (SFM) method starting with KPS performance to boost quality improvements in its 10 plants. After the implementation, the managers shared their thoughts with us about the project:

- 'The initial phase of the SFM implementation involved deploying the six performance metrics for our 10 plants, starting with KPS performance. The participation of the plant manager who would be using SFM was essential to the success of the project.'

- 'As first-line managers we have to work with scoreboards designed by top managers who do not have operations at the forefront of their mind. Adopting the SFM bottom-up approach meant that we would have a business process management system that fits our exact requirements.'

- 'Development of performance metrics and KPIs proceeded quickly, in large part because of the simplicity and no-frills approach of the method, which rapidly led to the configuration of the ideal scoreboard for us. These metrics were developed by the middle and first-line managers.'

- 'The SFM method made it easy for us to generate field indicators from the six key performance indicators.'

- 'We were trained and assisted by an SFM expert who has extensive experience in building performance management scoreboards.'

- 'The three first performance projects we selected as a priority – KPS, people responsibility level (PRL) and return on critical resource (RCR) – were completed in six weeks, with most of that time devoted to defining the KPIs required for measuring the performance indicators.'

- 'Today, all our 10 plants are using the SFM method for profitable growth, with special focus on KPS performance. The key projects of the 10 plant directors were different, but the focus was the same: one big improvement project constantly running and carefully monitored by indicators specifying availability, milestones, net present value, etc.'

- 'The six figure scoreboard gives us a more accurate view of the impact of our operations on the strategy of our company. We can use this information to identify priorities and to help identify specific problems that may influence financial results in the long term. They have allowed first-line managers to identify a correlation between their efforts and the success of our company.'

- 'The successful deployment of SFM at the pilot plant also made a compelling case to all the other plants. Thanks to the knowledge and training we have gained through the SFM expert at the pilot plant we are developing the scoreboard of the other plants internally.'

- 'Those six performance indicators are aggregated results. They force us to break down the information silos in our company, as, for example, the KPS performance metrics request that different units provide their own data to build the scoreboard.'

Summary

Your sustainable, profitable growth is now on track, with the six KPIs on display, measuring and improving.

What's next

In the next chapter, we turn to action: how to get started.

Getting started

How to start

When no or incomplete methodology is used, important issues are missed or forgotten. If this happens, you are no longer controlling the situation and are relying on luck. This is a dangerous position for your organization, because it means that you are not aware of your weaknesses, blindly take decisions, and stress certain issues without acknowledging the whole picture.

The six figure method will enable you to measure and manage your organization's performance in a structured and balanced way. All strategic aspects will be covered, and you will have access to a global view of the organization.

Where should you begin?

The six figure management method can be applied on three different levels: you as an individual, your team and your organization.

Begin by using the six figures on something that you know well and manage daily: yourself. Decide which are the six figures of your professional activity, measure them and manage your professional life accordingly. After becoming familiar with this method, continue by scaling it up to your team and finally to your organization.

As soon as this method and its advantages are clear, decide within your team on the six figures corresponding to your situation. Create a project to implement and develop a performance dashboard based on these KPIs. Be sure to name a KPI owner for each indicator and delegate actions and responsibilities to this person.

Figure 9.1 shows an example of how organizations implement the SFM method in four simple steps.

FIGURE 9.1 The SFM at work: an example

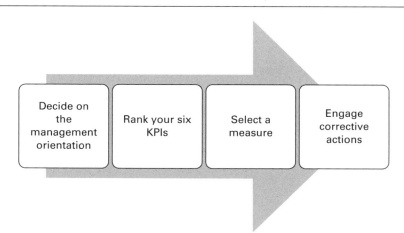

The first and key thing to do is to decide on the management orientation by asking a few easy but insightful questions:

- What orientation do we want to give to our management in the coming quarters?
- Do growth and innovation come first, with actions to improve our sales from new sources (SFN) performance?
- Do customers and the market come first, with actions to improve our time facing customers (TFC) performance? (See Figure 9.2.)

FIGURE 9.2   When customers come first

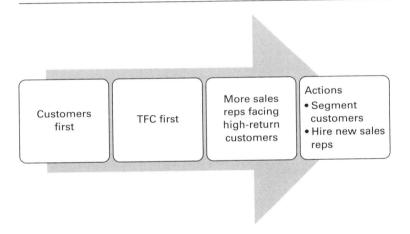

- Do cost leadership and operational excellence come first, with actions to improve our gains from processes (GFP) performance?
- Do employees and motivation come first, with actions to improve our people responsibility level (PRL) performance?
- Do profitability and cash come first, with actions to improve our return on critical resource (RCR) performance?
- Do leadership and change come first, with actions to improve our key project status (KPS) performance?

Why not start at your own personal level?

A smart idea that executives often apply in order to feel comfortable with the SFM method is try it out on themselves as one-person organizations (see Figure 9.3). They can then scale it up to their teams and even their organizations.

FIGURE 9.3   How to deploy the SFM programme

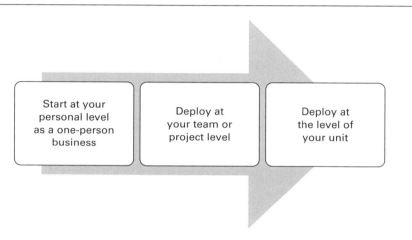

We now discuss some examples of the six performance measurements at the different levels. If, as a manager, you start to measure and improve your own individual six figures, it will always have a positive bottom-up impact on the six performance figures of your team and organization.

Examples of SFN performance measurements

- *When applied at the individual level*: new responsibilities are obtained thanks to newly acquired competencies and certifications.
- *When applied at the team level*: new budgets are obtained thanks to new business plans.

- *When applied at the business unit level:* new revenues are generated from new products.

Examples of TFC performance measurement

- *When applied at the individual level:* hours per week facing the boss.
- *When applied at the team level:* hours per week in front of internal customers, the users of the outputs.
- *When applied at the business unit level:* hours per week per salesperson in front of potential customers.

Examples of GFP performance measurement

- *When applied at the individual level:* number of target tasks processed as an action checklist and then delegated to collaborators.
- *When applied at the team level:* number of team processes with a completed process master document and running in an automated way.
- *When applied at the business unit level:* cost gains generated by processing target activities.

Examples of PRL performance measurement

- *When applied at the individual level:* tangible increase in personal responsibilities in one year.
- *When applied at the team level:* increase in financial amounts that do not need a second signature as part of the responsibilities of key team members.
- *When applied at the business unit level:* number of AAA employees promoted within one year of the evaluation.

Examples of RCR performance measurement

- *When applied at the individual level:* net income per working hour.
- *When applied at the team level:* economic added value per manager.
- *When applied at the business unit level:* return per customer segment.

Examples of KPS performance measurement

- *When applied at the individual level:* next deliverable on time for a career project.
- *When applied at the team level:* joint team scoreboard project completed by a certain date.
- *When applied at the business unit level:* time to market for new product development reduced by 20 per cent.

FIGURE 9.4   From KPIs to measures to actions

Orders from new customer segments +15%	3 hours per day facing franchisee prospects	Reduce production costs by 2%
Opening three POS in NJ	Hiring one assistant for four reps	Identify a process director per process
SFN	TFC	GFP
Increase the AAA managers' budget by 50%	Increase average POS profit per square metre by 5%	Next deliverable on specification and on time
Evaluate all managers within three months	Close the three laggards within a month	Increase the budget for the new POS by 10%
PRL	RCR	KPS

CASE STUDY 9.1 A US apparel retail business

A US apparel retail business, after developing a market share strategy, wants to return to profitable growth using the scoreboard of the SFM method.

Here is the SFM process followed by this thriving company. At the kick-off seminar, the questions that the SFM consultant asked the managing team were simple and practical:

- *Step 1: Growth results with sales from new sources.* Where can you find the greatest growth space, in what region and with what customer segments?

- *Step 2: Growth activities with time facing potential franchisees and resellers.* Who will best support your growth: your own sales point, your franchisees, potential master franchisees, top resellers or large distributors?

- *Step 3: Financing the growth effort with gains from processes.* Can you make some resources available for your growth effort by reorganizing your processes, eg abandoning less profitable activities, subcontracting, automation, etc?

- *Step 4: Staffing the growth projects with the best people.* Who are your AAA managers? Can you afford to pay them more on performance, ie on the improvement of their SFM indicators?

- *Step 5: Check that this growth stays profitable with return on critical resource indicators.* What is your most critical resource? How will you measure its return, eg as profitability rates, occupation rates, etc?

- *Step 6: Lead the growth project with key project status indicators.* How will you visualize and lead this key project to focus all team members on it?

Some tips for success

- Be clear and consistent and communicate thoroughly throughout your organization.
- Make sure that your strategy is aligned to the six objectives and vice versa.
- Engage your employees in the process and motivate them by using an incentive programme based on the performance of the six figures.
- Establish clear targets and thresholds for defining the criticality of each issue: red, amber and green traffic lights.
- Create an intuitive dashboard with the data and results that you have obtained.
- Create scorecards to depict graphically the history of each performance indicator.
- Make sure that the measurements are followed by corrective actions.
- Once the process is put in place, automate it so that you instantly have your results every quarter.

Start from a priority

Both the ranking and the measurement of the six performance indicators can be different according to your current priorities. The priority of 'Improve profit' will obviously trigger different measures on the SFM scoreboard than will the priority of 'Increase market share' or 'Boost innovation', but it's not in the scope of this book to develop this subject.

Figure 9.5 shows an example of how the six figures are configured in a case where the priority is 'Improve profit'. Figure 9.6 shows the choices for action for each of the six figures in a case where the priority is 'Boost innovation'.

FIGURE 9.5   Improving profit

SFN	• Increase sales of new high-margin products • Increase sales to new high-margin customers • Increase sales from new high-margin channels
TFC	• Increase the sales rep hours per day facing the most profitable customers • Increase the number of sales reps dedicated to the most profitable customers
GFP	• Reduce activity costs by processing them • Improve the streamline index for the most costly processes • Subcontract, delocalize and digitalize more activities
PRL	• Allocate more budget to the most cost-conscious employees
RCR	• Increase the utilization rate of your most expensive resource
KPS	• Engage a major cost leadership project

FIGURE 9.6   Boosting innovation

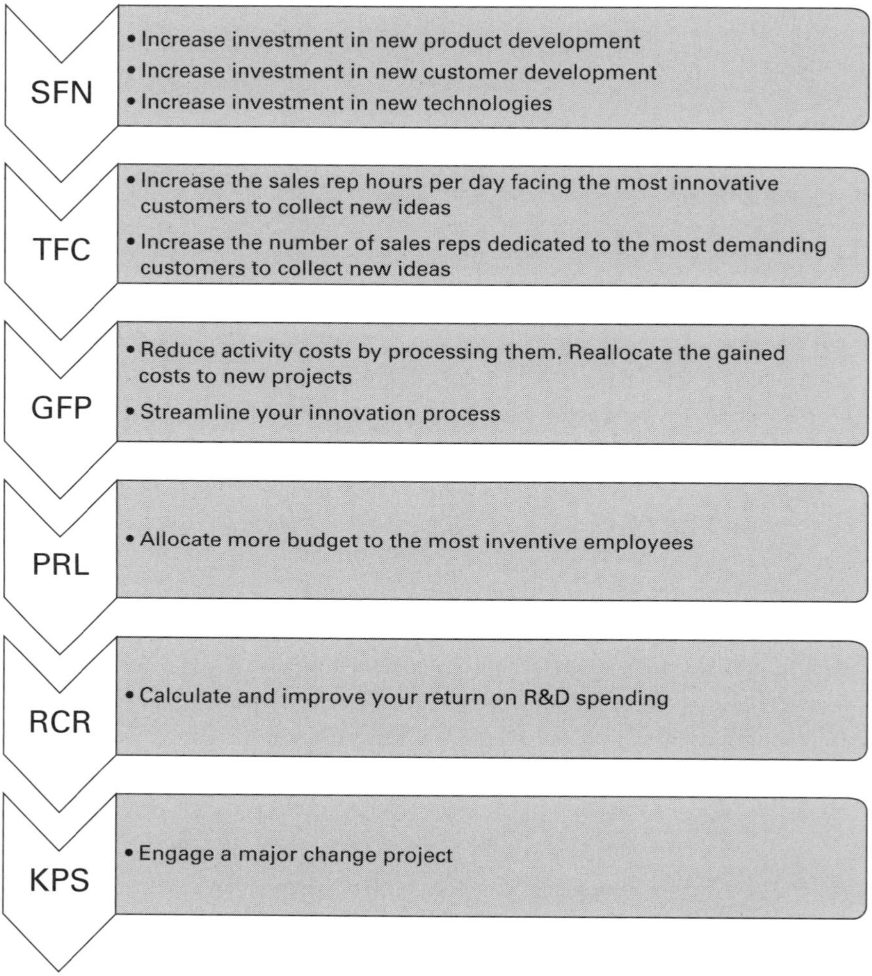

SFN
- Increase investment in new product development
- Increase investment in new customer development
- Increase investment in new technologies

TFC
- Increase the sales rep hours per day facing the most innovative customers to collect new ideas
- Increase the number of sales reps dedicated to the most demanding customers to collect new ideas

GFP
- Reduce activity costs by processing them. Reallocate the gained costs to new projects
- Streamline your innovation process

PRL
- Allocate more budget to the most inventive employees

RCR
- Calculate and improve your return on R&D spending

KPS
- Engage a major change project

How do managers tailor SFM to the strategic and environmental context?

The SFM method seems rigid. It prescribes only six well-defined KPIs that are used in all circumstances. Yet experience shows that managers quickly adapt the method to changes in their environment. There are two ways managers make the method more flexible.

First, managers prioritize the six KPIs to fit their unique strategic situation. If, for example, adaptation to the environment and competitors requires a reduction in costs and delays, GFP performance is placed at the centre of the dashboard. It will be aligned with different measurements. It will be more detailed, with measurements of quicker transformation of activities into processes, measurements of indexes of process complexity, and so on. From the standpoint of KPS performance, the need to reduce costs will be translated by the fact that the replacement of the project is usually followed by a project on cost reduction. The four other KPIs may no longer be displayed at this responsibility level, to emphasize this cost reduction priority.

Second, managers change the measurements that measure the KPIs. For example, if the environment requires that managers be more innovative in a particular area of competition, the SFN performance measurements will be changed. For example, the 'sale of new products' measurement will be replaced by the 'sales from new clients' measurement on the dashboards. Or, if the environment requires that an organization be quicker, without requiring cost reductions, the GFP performance measurements will be changed by, for example, replacing 'key cost reduction' with 'key delay reduction' as the organization's GFP performance measurement.

Help in getting started

The software solution

The six figure application is an intuitive and highly valuable plug-in solution for your business. It consists of a software program capable of generating a performance cockpit based on your existing data. An easy-to-use graphical user interface can take your preferred options for measurement periodicity, calculation methods and data source.

Once installed by our business technology specialist, the six figures are integrated inside your reporting. On demand, the six figure application will perform a query on your existing database solution, whether it's SAP, Oracle or whatever.

The action part of SFM: the INDIRA website

If you want the growth initiated by SFM to be sustainable, you should root it at team and at manager level. You can achieve that with INDIRA©. This website is a new-generation, objective-oriented enterprise social network that drives all employees to get involved with results, sharing their knowledge, their time-sheets and their contacts.

The SFM business application for INDIRA includes an SFM dashboard function, project portfolio function and social network function.

How it works

1 Ask all first-line managers to volunteer for their own local, team SFM micro-project.

2 Allocate to each SFM micro-project a page on INDIRA, the collaborative intranet website included with the SFM application.

3 Request that each first-line manager fills in the questionnaires on their own INDIRA web page, structured to make it searchable by the INDIRA search engine.

4 Look at the consolidated results. All local SFM micro-projects now contribute to enterprise-wide long-term growth.

FIGURE 9.7   How executives make their SFM strategy happen: the INDIRA website is an emerging favourite

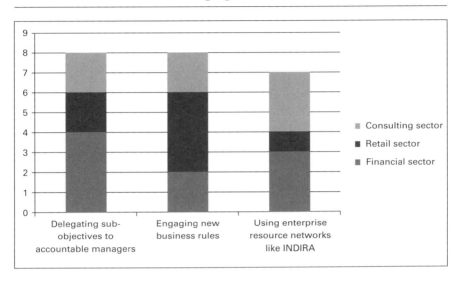

FIGURE 9.8   Building the SFM task force with INDIRA

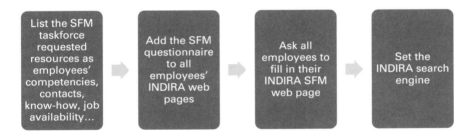

The SFM application for INDIRA: piloting the implementation project at a major Canadian IT services company

The implementation project proceeded as follows over nine months:

1 set project growth goals as SFN target values;

2 motivate people with PRL, select the best people, and give them more;

3 give them RCR objectives to free cash for SFN;

4 free resources with GFP: automate, subcontract, delocalize, and abandon less profitable activities;

5 increase TFC to explore new markets for SFN;

6 follow the project with KPS.

Testimonial: The CEO of a major Canadian IT consulting company

'SFM is the application that will finally give us a return on our intranet, dashboard and balanced scorecard investments.'

How to make things happen with INDIRA

Figures 9.9, 9.10 and 9.11 show how objectives are cascaded to the relevant managers.

FIGURE 9.9   INDIRA Objective Reacher application at work during an innovation campaign, offering cascaded objectives to profiled managers

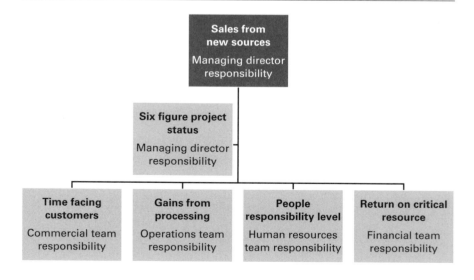

FIGURE 9.10 INDIRA Objective Reacher application at work during a cost-cutting campaign, offering cascaded objectives to profiled managers

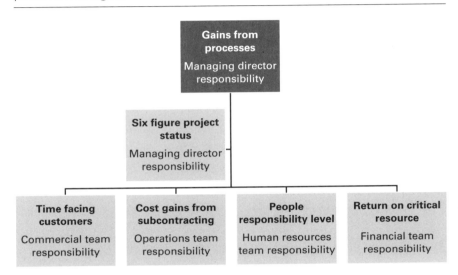

FIGURE 9.11 INDIRA Objective Reacher at work during a sales increase campaign, offering cascaded objectives to profiled managers

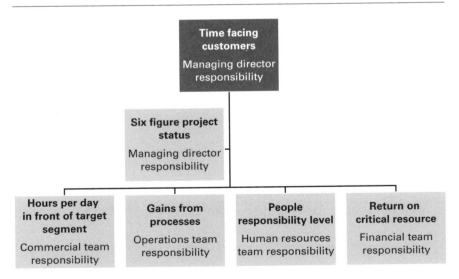

A typical INDIRA Objective Reacher dialog box on the personal web page of a profiled manager might look like this:

INDIRA: Peter, do you want to concur with the objective 'Sales from new customers at 15%'?

Peter: Yes. I can contribute to this objective with the following resources on my INDIRA web page:

- my hot news on potential new customers;
- my contacts with prospects;
- my agenda dedicated to new customers;
- my competencies that can help;
- the status of my local projects that can contribute to this objective;
- my FAQ list related to this objective.

FIGURE 9.12   The INDIRA Objective Reacher application, from measurements to growth

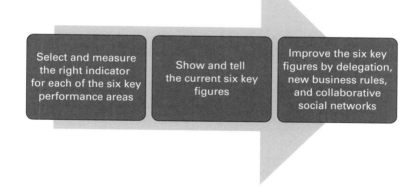

Select and measure the right indicator for each of the six key performance areas

Show and tell the current six key figures

Improve the six key figures by delegation, new business rules, and collaborative social networks

To improve your six key figures, the INDIRA case memory proposes the business rules that managers frequently apply. An example using the people responsibility level is shown in Figure 9.13.

FIGURE 9.13   A PRL example

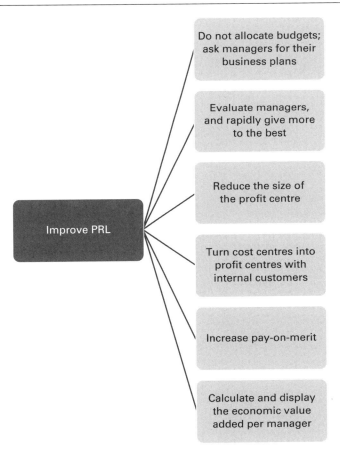

FIGURE 9.14 A typical feature of the INDIRA Objective Reacher application, cascading the right sub-objectives to the right person, at the right moment, with the right incentives

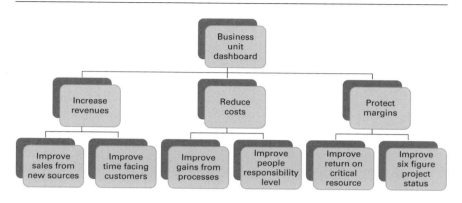

An example of the INDIRA Objective Reacher application when applied to the SFM method

INDIRA asks managers to answer the key questions on what is critical for them this quarter:

- *Sales from new sources:* Focus on what new product, which new customers or which new processes?

- *Time facing customers:* What time? What customers?

- *Gains from processes:* What gains? What processes?

- *People responsibility level:* Which people? What responsibilities?

- *Return on critical resource:* What resource? What return?

- *Key project status:* What project? What quarterly deliverable?

For more information, go to **www.indiraweb.com.**

The seminar

A six figure seminar is available on request. Management experts will train you and your team on how to tailor the six figure method to your own business. It's a smart shortcut to save time and money and rely on our built expertise to add value to your organization.

Boost your team and your results

Dedicate one intensive day to your unit, to giving it a new impetus and increasing its effectiveness and profitability. The goal is for your team, at the end of the day, to come to an agreement on a scoreboard of six key performance indicators, with objectives of quarterly progress.

A detailed programme for the day

We have experience of leading team seminars for 200 or more people. Here is how to organize the day.

Morning: making choices

Among the six key performance areas, which are your priorities? Innovation with SFN? Income and sales with TFC? Cost cutting and improvement of quality with GFP? The motivation of staff with PRL? Profitability improvements with RCR? A radical change with KPS?

How will you measure your priority performance area? Which measurable indicators will you choose for each one of your three priority performance areas? For example, if you choose SFN as your priority, which types of income are most important for you and which type of innovation is most important for you: new products, new customers or new processes?

Afternoon: engaging actions

How will you set the objectives of the selected indicators? Which calculable target will you fix quarterly for each one of these three indicators? Compared to your past? Compared to your competitors? Compared to the standards of your industry?

How will you achieve these goals and improve your perform-ance? For each of the six performance indicators, you will find several methods to improve them. Choose one or two. Draw up a precise project for each one, with a project director and a precise plan of the project.

How will you motivate your staff to follow you? How will you automate your new scoreboard?

For more information, go to **www.six-figuremanager.com/en/**.

Conclusion: what's next

1 Start by applying your scoreboard to yourself as a one-person business.

2 Then apply your scoreboard to your business priority: boosting innovation, regaining profitability, etc.

3 Get some starting help by attending a six figure seminar with your team.

Conclusion
Key points of the SFM method

The golden rule of a business that works

If you measure, compare and display visibly, on walls and screens, to the right people the six figures that should drive your organization, your organization will thrive.

Below we set out what we have learnt from our customers, in the course of 10 years, when helping them to design their scoreboards.

How to improve your sales from new sources performance

1 Decide on the 'new' that is really strategic for you: new products, or new customers, or new processes.

2 Organize the collection of new ideas from customers, suppliers and employees by the organization of a true innovation process.

3 Copy a good idea from a competitor, improve the idea, and beat the competitor by investing more money or engaging more salespeople than it can.

How to improve your time facing customers performance

1 Increase staff facing customers, and decrease staff in the back office.

2 Delegate the operations to invest in marketing.

3 Sell first; produce after.

How to improve your gains from processes performance

1 Do not allow any activities apart from a clear project or a well-defined process.

2 Transform successful projects into processes quickly.

3 Automate, subcontract and delocalize processes, at the target quality level, to reduce costs and delays.

How to improve your people responsibility level performance

1 Increase the responsibilities, budgets and means entrusted to your best people as fast as you can.
2 Do not allocate any more budgets; ask the people in charge for business plans.
3 Reward according to achieved goals, chosen by the people in charge themselves.

How to improve your return on critical resource performance

1 Measure everything; always be aware of all your profitability per project, per process, per unit, per manager, per customer segment and so on.
2 Each year, give up your least profitable 5 per cent of activities, customers, processes, suppliers and so on.
3 Finance your new activities by the gains from dropping less profitable activities.

How to improve your key project status performance

1 Choose only one major change project, which will mark your leadership. Concentrate on this project, and delegate routines and processes to your number two.
2 Fill out the master document of the project precisely, and entrust it to a senior project manager.
3 Check each quarter personally to confirm whether the main deliverable has been produced on time and to your standards.

REFERENCES

Aguinis, Herman (2009) *Performance Management*, 2nd edn, Prentice Hall/ Pearson Education, Upper Saddle River, NJ

Armstrong, Michael (2006) *Performance Management: Key strategies and practical guidelines*, Kogan Page, London

Beine, Martin (2006) *Empowerment and Innovation: Managers, principles and reflective practice*, Edward Elgar, Cheltenham

Georges, Patrick M (2004) *Management Cockpit: Essential scoreboards*, Eyrolles, Paris

Georges, Patrick M and Sinzig, Werner (2000) The Management Cockpit: The human interface for management software – reviewing 50 user sites over 10 years of experience, *Wirtschaftsinformatik*, **42** (2), pp 134–36

Griffin, Ricky W (2005) *Management*, Houghton Mifflin, Boston, MA

Hadedoom, John and Cloodt, Myriam (2003) Measuring innovative performance: Is there an advantage in using multiple indicators?, *Research Policy*, **32** (8), September, pp 1365–79

Hoffmann, Carl, Lesser, Eric and Ringo, Tim (2012) *Calculating Success: How the new workplace analytics will revitalize your organization*, Harvard Business School Publishing, Boston, MA

Jeston, John and Nelis, Johan (2008) *Business Process Management: Practical guidelines to successful implementations*, 2nd edn, Elsevier, Oxford

Johnston, R, Brignall, S and Fitzgerald, L (2002) 'Good enough' performance measurement: A trade-off between activity and action, *Journal of the Operational Research Society*, **53** (3), March, Part Special Issue: Performance Management, pp 256–62

Kaplan, Robert S (2009) *Measuring Performance*, Harvard Business School Publishing, Boston, MA

Kaplan, Robert S and Norton, David P (1992) The balanced scorecard: Measures that drive performance, *Harvard Business Review*, January– February

Kaplan, Robert S and Norton, David P (1996) Using the balanced scorecard as a strategic system, *Harvard Business Review*, January–February

Kroll, Mark *et al* (1997) Form of control: A critical determinant of acquisition performance and CEO rewards, *Strategic Management Journal*, **18** (2), pp 85–96

Lebas, Michel (1995) Performance measurement and performance management, *International Journal of Production Economics*, **41**, October, pp 23–35

Montague, Read (2006) *How We Make Decisions*, Penguin Science, East Rutherford, NJ

Nykamp, Melinda (2001) *The Customer Differential*, Amacom, New York

Otley, David (1999) Performance management: a framework for management control systems research, *Management Accounting Research*, **10** (4), December, pp 363–82

Parmenter, David (2009) *Key Performance Indicators: Developing, implementing and using winning KPIs*, 2nd edn, Wiley, Hoboken, NJ

Phillips, Jack, Phillips, Patti and Ray, Rebecca (2012) *Measuring Leadership Development: Quantify your program's impact and ROI on organizational performance*, McGraw-Hill, New York.

Pinker, Steven (1999) *How the Mind Works*, W W Norton, New York

Smith, K H (2005) *Measuring Innovation*, Oxford University Press, Oxford

Taylor, William (1994) Control in an age of chaos, *Harvard Business Review*, November–December, pp 64–70

Walker, Richard M, Jeannes, Emma and Rowlands, Robert (2002) *Measuring Innovation: Applying the literature-based innovation output indicator to public services*, Blackwell, Oxford

Walsh, Ciaran (1996) *Key Management Ratios*, Pitman Publishing, London

INDEX

NB: page numbers in *italic* indicate figures or tables